Inspirations
From the Mind of God
to the
Heart
of a
Believer

Inspirations From the Mind of God to the Heart of a Believer

Devotional Readings with Tips for Understanding and Coping with Life's Challenges.

Marlene D. Barnes-Hunter

XULON PRESS

Xulon Press
2301 Lucien Way #415
Maitland, FL 32751
407.339.4217
www.xulonpress.com

© 2019 by Marlene D. Barnes-Hunter
2nd Edition April 2020

All rights reserved solely by the author. The author guarantees all contents are original and do not infringe upon the legal rights of any other person or work. No part of this book may be reproduced in any form without the permission of the author. The views expressed in this book are not necessarily those of the publisher.

Unless otherwise indicated, Scripture quotations taken from the Holy Bible, New International Version (NIV). Copyright © 1973, 1978, 1984, 2011 by Biblica, Inc.™. Used by permission. All rights reserved.

Scripture quotations taken from the King James Version (KJV) – *public domain*.

Printed in the United States of America.

ISBN-13: 978-1-5456-7134-4

Table of Contents

Week 1 1
    What Is Strength? 1
    Walking in Your Destiny 3

Week 2 4
    Destiny 4
    Walking in God's Will 6

Week 3 8
    Victory 8
    The P.O.S of God 10
    Jesus, The Greatest Husband 11

Week 4 14
    Submit 14
    Purify Me, O God 15

Week 5 16
    You Are My Refuge and Strength 16
    Preserve Me 17

Week 6 18
    Prosperity 18
    What Is Meekness? 20

Week 7 22
    Meekness Is 22
    Pray 24

Week 8 26
   Living A Lifestyle of Praise 26
   Light 29

Week 9 30
   Hallelujah Anyhow 30
   Declaration of God's Elect Lady................... 32

Week 10 34
   Forgiveness is 34
   GRACE... 36

Week 11 37
   CHANGE 37
   Consecrate Your Members 38

Week 12 40
   I am God's Child.................................. 40
   ANGER... 42

Week 13 43
   Show Me An Angry Person........................... 43
   Emotional Abuse Is Not of God 46
   What Will You Do with This Man Jesus?............. 48

Week 14 51
   WAIT.. 51
   The Lord Is My Protection 53
   The Glory of Them All 55

Week 15 57
   STEWARDSHIP....................................... 57
   SATISFACTION...................................... 59
   PEACE 61

Week 16 62
Obedience 62
M.A.N. 64
The Truth About Fatherhood. 66

Week 17 67
Man Born of Woman Is Full of Trouble 67
Man: The Human Race 68
Love Is 70

Week 18 72
Love Never Fails. 72
Beloved 73
Lover.. 74

Week 19 75
Your Love Constrains Me and Restrains Me 75
Jesus Is the Gate 77
I Shall Prevail 78

Week 20 79
Jesus, I'm in Need...................................... 79
HOPE 81
Humility Is The Key 82

Week 21 84
HONOR 84
Happiness Is 85
Guide Me 87

Week 22 89
God Is a God of New Beginnings..................... 89
Give God a Chance in Your Life...................... 90
Fragrance.. 92

Week 23 .... **93**
   Passion 93
   Fishers of Men 95
   Integrity.. 96

Week 24 .... **97**
   Declaration of a Woman of Integrity 97
   Alone with God...................................... 99
   Breakthrough.. 101

Week 25 .... **102**
   Bring Us Down Lord 102
   Are You Ready? 104
   The Intangible 106

Week 26 .... **108**
   You Are the Glory and the Lifter of My Head 108
   Declaration of God's Glory in Your Life 110
   Stand 111

Week 27 .... **112**
   Thanks 112
   Surrender... 113

Week 28 .... **114**
   The Blood of Jesus 114
   Easter Is for Our Redemption 116

Week 29 .... **117**
   God is My Vindicator 117
   Being Secure in Christ Guarantees Success 119

Week 30 .... **121**
   Words 121
   Tongue.. 122

Week 31 .... **123**
    The Tongue Is Controlled by the Speaker. 123
    Anointing 125

Week 32 .... **127**
    Wake Up 127
    Successful Transition Takes Time. 128

Week 33 .... **130**
    Holy Spirit You Are Welcome in My Life 130
    Woman 132
    Declaration of Who I Am 133

Week 34 .... **135**
    Discipline 135
    Tears 137

Week 35 .... **139**
    Thoughts 139
    Offense 141

Week 36 .... **142**
    Serve God 142
    How to Invoke Respect. 143

Week 37 .... **144**
    Accountability. 144
    Are You a Giver or a Taker? 146

Week 38 .... **148**
    His Majesty. 148
    The Sanctuary of God. 150

Week 39 .... **152**
    Enter In His Presence 152
    Fault-Finding. 154

Week 40 .... **156**
    Divert Me, O God 156
    Redemption 158

Week 41 .... **160**
    Revival 160
    Helper 162

Week 42 .... **163**
    The Journey Is Rough, But 163
    Clean Hands 165

Week 43 .... **167**
    The Leviathan Spirit 167
    Mind-Readers 170

Week 44 .... **172**
    Substance 172
    Secure Your Joy 174

Week 45 .... **175**
    T-I-M-E 175
    My Times Are in Your Hands 176

Week 46 .... **177**
    Don't Sweat the Small Stuff 177
    Sanctification Is 178

Week 47 .... **180**
    Focus on the Future 180
    Never Give Up, You Are Precious 182

Week 48 .... **184**
    Be Still and Know That He Is God 184
    Faith Is 186

Week 49 .... **188**
   God Is Able 188
   Worship, Evangelism, Discipleship 190

Week 50 .... **192**
   What Is Freedom? 192
   Be Still My Soul 195

Week 51 .... **197**
   God Can Heal the Broken Heart 197
   Trust God Always 199

Week 52 .... **201**
   You Can Depend on God 201
   You Are Lord God Almighty 203
   Stay on Track 205
   Deliverance 207
   Patience 209
   The In-Between Times 211

INTRODUCTION

EVERY STAGE OF LIFE COMES WITH ITS CHALlenges, from the day we were born until we take our last breath. The question is, "How will we address each challenge?" Will we rollover and die or resort to a subculture that will push us into a depressive mood of hopelessness? <u>Or</u> will we make the decision to reach out to our Creator and find refuge in Him.

God will provide us with hope, strength and the direction we need. In Him there is a reservoir of a never-ending, refreshing stream of living water that we can step into for every challenge that life brings.

My hope for every reader of this poetic book of inspirations — those who are seeking refuge, resolutions and answers to life's challenges, and an intimate relationship with Jesus — is that he or she will find God's presence and experience a refreshing revival, deliverance and sweet peace.

WEEK 1

WHAT IS STRENGTH?

Strength
is the ability expressed through God's love
to smile genuinely at someone whom you've toiled
hard and long for, even though that someone looks at
you and says
"You've done nothing for me."

Strength
is God allowing you to look into the eyes
of someone who stole something
precious from you and saying, to that someone,
"God loves you, no matter what you've done."

Strength
is the Holy Spirit directing us to say with sincerity,
"I still care for you," to a loved one
whom you thought loved you but criticizes and gossips
about you.

Strength
is the power of God enabling you to bounce back
with more strength after you've
had 24 hours of punching, stabbing and being picked on nonstop.

Strength
is the breath and grace of God waking you up in the morning
and prompting
you to say with reality, "I've done everything that is
humanly possible and it hasn't worked, but let me try this,
it might work."

Strength
is God's love multiplied in you and causes you to say to your enemies "I love you with the love of God."

2 Corinthians 12:9 states, "And He said unto me, 'My grace is sufficient for you, for my strength is made perfect in weakness.'"

(Read also, Exodus 15:2; Psalm 18:32-33; Joel 3:10; 1John 2:14.)

Prayer

My Lord and Master, when I am weak you make me strong. I know I can depend on you because I can do nothing without you. I thank you for your supernatural strength. Amen!

Walking in Your Destiny

Delving into that place where God

Established the path for your

Sanctified spirit and soul, where you can

Truly see God as your source and guide, as He

Inspires you to carry out the GREAT COMMISSION where

No-one who meets you will go by, without a touch from

Your gifts, for the honor and glory of God.

Ephesians 1:2–6 (NIV) states, "Grace be to you, and peace, from God our Father, and from the Lord Jesus Christ. Blessed be the God and Father of our Lord Jesus Christ, who hath blessed us with all spiritual blessings in heavenly places in Christ. For He hath chosen us in him before the creation of the world, that we should be holy and without blame before him. In love he predestinated us unto the adoption of children by Jesus Christ to himself, according to the good pleasure of his will, To the praise of the glory of his grace, where-in he hath made us accepted in the beloved."

(See also, Romans 8:3.)

Prayer

Father, you are the almighty God and there is none other. I appreciate You for who You are. Thank you for ordering my steps. Please cause me to be sensitive to Your voice so that I will do what You want me to do. It is in the strong name Jesus, I pray. Amen!

WEEK 2

DESTINY

Determination that takes you on

Eagles wings to a realm of

Satisfaction where you will be provided with the attitude and spirit of

Teachability which will cause you to live a life of

Integrity for God to elevate you to

Noteworthiness and heavenly places, as you

Yield to His leading.

Determination: A resolution, settlement or purpose in your mind or heart.

1 Corinthians 2:2, "For I am determined to know anything among you, save Jesus Christ and Him, crucified."

Eagles wings: "…you have seen how I bear you on eagles wings and brought you to myself." Exodus 19:4. God desires intimacy with His people.

Sanctification: Separation from evil to give of oneself unreservedly to God.

1 Corinthians 6:9–11 and Romans 8:13–16.

A process of obedience to God's word and following the examples of Christ. The Holy Spirit is the Agent that Sanctifies.

Teachability: Possessing the attitude to be taught Psalm 25:4, 27:11; Job 3:33.

Integrity: Soundness of character, which causes an individual to not compromise Godly principles. Proverbs 20:7; Psalm 25:21.

Noteworthiness: Remarkable and worthy of notice. Ephesians 1: 3-5, 20

Yield to His leading: Obedience to God's voice/word, submitting to His commands. Luke 1:6: "And they were both righteous before God, walking in all the commandments and ordinances of the Lord blameless.

Luke 23: 49, 55-56 (NIV) states, "And all his acquaintance, and the women that followed him from Galilee, stood afar off, beholding these things ... And the women also which came with him from Galilee, followed after, and beheld the sepulcher, and how his body was laid. And they returned and prepared spices and ointments; and rested the sabbath day according to the commandment."

Read also, Romans 12: 1-2.

<u>Prayer</u>
My great God, worthy are you to receive honor, glory and majesty. I glorify you because you planned my destiny to represent you while I live on this earth. Grant me the spirit of obedience so that I will walk in Your integrity.

WALKING IN GOD'S WILL

Wisdom – The ability to discern modes of action in order
      to view their results;
      The insight into the true nature of things
      Penetrating consideration which precedes an action.

Illumination – To give light;
      To shine forth; spiritual enlightenment

Love – To express the essential nature of God.
      Christian love has God for its primary object and expresses itself first of all in implicit obedience to His commandments. Love is seen in deeds.

Long-suffering – Forbearance, patience to bear long, endurance
      To be "long tempered" (self-controlled) that quality of self-restraint in the face of provocation, which does not hastily retaliate or promptly punish; it is the opposite of anger, and is associated with mercy and used of God. Enveloped with patience, the quality that does not surrender to circumstances or succumbs under trial, it is the opposite of despondency and associated with hope.

Wisdom: James 1:5; (KJV) states, "If any of you lacks wisdom, he should ask God, Who gives generously to all without finding fault, and it will be given to him".

(See also, James 3:17; Proverbs 3:13, 4:5–13; Ephesians 1:17, 7–9; 5:15; Colossians 2:1–3; 2 Timothy 3:15; 1Corinthians 4:10.)

Illuminate: Revelation 22:5 (NIV) states, "There will be no more night. They will not need the light of a lamp or the light of the sun, for the Lord God will give them light. And they will reign for ever and ever."

(See also, Ephesians 1:18, 5:14, 3:9; Hebrews 6:4; 1 Corinthians 4:5; John 1:14, 5:9, 3:19, 8:12, 9:5, 12:35–36, 46.)

Love: John 17:26 (NIV), "I have made you known to them, and will continue to make you known in order that the love you have for me may be in them and that I may be in them and that I myself may be in them."

(See also John 3:16, 14:21, 13:37, 4:15, 12 13; 1 John 4:8; 1 Thessalonians 3:12; 1 Corinthians 16:14; 2 Peter 1:7; 2 Corinthians 5:14; Galatians 5:22; Ephesians 2:4, 3:19, 5:22)."

Long-suffering: Thessalonians 5:14–15 (NIV) states, "And we urge you, brothers warn those who idle, encourage the timid, help the weak, be patient with everyone. Make sure that nobody pays back wrong for wrong, but always try to be kind to each other and to everyone else."

(See also, Exodus 34:6; Romans 2:4; 1 Peter 3:20; 2 Peter 1:3–7; James 5:11.)

Definitions: Vine's Complete Expository Dictionary

<u>Prayer</u>

Dear Lord, I thank you very much that you cause me to experience the light of life – Jesus. Teach me wisdom to recognize those things that reflect your character, so that I will make the right decisions in every area of my life. In Jesus' name I pray. Amen.

WEEK 3

VICTORY

Venture

Into a

Celebration of Praise to Jehovah in order to

Triumph and

Overcome the

Rudiments of the

Yoke of bondage to things that fade and die.

VICTORY— (1) Final and complete defeat of the enemy in a military engagement.

(2) Any successful struggle against an opponent or obstacle.
Concise American Heritage Dictionary

(3) To conquer, to overcome
Vine's Complete Expository Dictionary

(4) The experience of a supernatural intervention from God that causes us to win in circumstances or struggles of the body, soul, or spirit
Holy Spirit revealed definition

1 Corinthians 15:53–55, 57–58 – Victory over death and the victor's shout

1 John 5:4–5 states, "For whatever is born of God overcomes the world: and this is the victory that overcomes the world, even our faith. Who is he that overcomes the world, but he that believeth that Jesus is the Son of God."

1 John 5:19 states, "For we know that we are of God, and the whole world lieth in wickedness."

WORLD – The order of man ruled governments temporal things/possessions/materialism.

> The present condition of human affairs (ungodly lifestyle, against the character of God) alienation from and opposition to God.

John 8:23 (NIV) states, "And He said unto them, ye are from beneath, I am from above, Ye are of this world; I am not of this world."

1 Corinthians 2:12 states, "Now we have received, not the spirit of the world, but the spirit which is of God; that we might know the things that are freely given to us of God."

Galatians 4:3 states, "…when we were children, we were in bondage under elements of the world."

<u>Prayer</u>

Jehovah, you are everything to me. Great is your faithfulness. I thank you very much that I am no longer in bondage to the elements of this world, because in you, I am victorious! In Jesus' name I pray. Amen.

The P.O.S. of God (Preservation, Overshadowing, Support)

When eaglets are learning to fly, the mother eagle gently nudges her babies out of the nest. If the eaglets make a mistake or start to fall, the mother eagle catches them safely. She is always watching the young eagles in case they need help, her help. God cares for us just like mother eagle cares for her babies.

Deuteronomy 32:11–12 states, "As an eagle stirs up her nest, flutters over her young around her wings, Taketh them and bears them on her wings; so the Lord alone did lead him, and there was no strange God with him."

God guarantees divine preservation, overshadowing and support for those who serve Him as God.

Divine Preservation – Deut. 6:24; Psalm 31:23; Psalm 37:28

Divine Overshadowing – Psalm 57:1; Exodus 33:22; Isaiah 51:16

Divine Support – Isaiah 41:10; Psalm 18:35

Isaiah 40:29 – He gives power and increases strength.

Deuteronomy 33:27 The eternal God is our refuge. Underneath are His everlasting arms..

Prayer
Lord, I love you because you are my protection. You carry me on eagle's wings, your wings—where there is no harm. Thank you for preserving, overshadowing and supporting me. No one else can do what you do for me. That's why I keep on going while I rest in your refuge. Underneath are His everlasting arms. In Jesus name I pray. Amen.

Jesus, The Greatest Husband

A Prayer of Adoration

Jesus, it's great being married to You because You are everything to me. Everything!

You are pure and without blemish, which assures me that I can be pure.

You are faithful. I can depend on You because You are always there. You said, you'll never leave me nor forsake me.

You are my present and my future, therefore, my hope is in You.

You've never lied to me because You are, "the Truth"..

You are my direction because You said, "I am the way."

You are consistent, you never waiver—the same yesterday, today and forever.

You are my Living Water, because from You, flows an eternal fountain that I can drink from when I am thirsty.

You are my Bread of Life, therefore, I will never be hungry.

You light up my life because there is no shadiness nor shadow of turning with You.

You are my peace and protection in this confused and unsafe world.

You are my source of joy and satisfaction, because in Your presence there is fullness of joy and pleasures for evermore.

You know me more than anyone else does, you understand me very well, especially when I try to explain myself to You, or at the moment when someone else misunderstands me.

You are my Provider because in you, are the riches of glory, so I lack nothing.

You are the Builder of my self-esteem, so I walk with confidence and with my head lifted.

Ever since You married me, my life has not been the same; that is the reason I give, my time, my talent, my all.

Jesus, I love You even more so because You adequately and efficiently fill the gaps

that earthly husbands struggle to fill or cannot fill.

I appreciate Your warm and tender caressing presence which is so overwhelmingly awesome and unexplainable.

Because You are my pride and joy, I will not hesitate to introduce You to those who have never met You.

Jesus, I certainly look forward to that great jubilation at Your banqueting table. O glorious day when the sun never sets!

Isaiah 54:5 (NIV) states, "For your maker is your husband – the Lord Almighty is his name— the holy One of Israel is your redeemer; he is called the God of all the Earth."

(Read also Psalm 19:7; 1John 4:18.)

<u>Prayer</u>

Dear Lord, I cherish You as my:
    Rose that never fades,
    Beautiful Lilly of the Valley,

Bright and Shining Star,
Bridge over troubled-water,
Deliverer,
Breath of Life,
Healer,
Serenity,
The Strength of my life,
True Love. In the name of Jesus. Amen

WEEK 4

SUBMIT

Separate yourself

Unconditionally and unreservedly for your Lord's purpose.

Bow your will and emotions to your

Maker, with

Intensity of heart and with a

Teachable spirit.

2 Corinthians 10:3–6 (NIV), "For though we live in the world, we do not wage wars as the world does. The weapons we fight with are not the weapons of the world. On the contrary, they have divine power to demolish strongholds. We demolish arguments and every pretension that sets itself up against the knowledge of God, and we take captive every thought to make it obedient to Christ. And we will be ready to punish every act of disobedience, once your obedience is complete."

(See also, 2 Corinthians 6:17; John 15:10; Romans 12:1-5; 2 Corinthians 10:3–6; Ephesians 5:20–33.)

Prayer

Awesome God, I give my all to you, unreservedly. You are my Creator, so I yearn for you today and always. As I come to you, cause me to lose myself and find it in you. Help me to submit to you, the areas of my life where I have struggles and challenges. When I am victorious, you alone will get the honor and the glory through Jesus, my Lord. Amen.

Purify Me, O God

Pour in me, your

Unconditional love to

Restore my soul.

Instill your spirit within me **and**

Fortify me with

Yourself, so that I'll be pure in my mind, soul and body.

1 Peter 1:22 (NIV) states, "Now that you have purified yourselves by obeying the truth so that you have sincere love for your brothers, love one another deeply from the heart."

(See also, James 4:8, 1 John 3:3.)

<u>Prayer</u>

Dearest Lord, my God, I give you my life, my will, my emotions because it is easy for me to relax in my comfort zones. Lord, you are the one who allows the Holy Spirit to show me and steer me away from those things and situations that are not like you.

Thank you for your love, which purifies through Jesus Christ. Amen.

WEEK 5

YOU ARE MY REFUGE AND STRENGTH

Redeeming Grace comes from my
Ever-present
Father, who
Ushers me under His wings of Protection and
Gives me an
Eternal resting place.

Strong Tower and
Teacher of those who hunger and thirst for
Righteousness welcomes those who seek to
Enter into His
Never-failing truth and glory.
God, who
Touches the heart, soul and spirit like no-one else,
He has conquered all principalities and wickedness on my behalf.

Psalm 9:9 (NIV) states, "The Lord is a refuge for the oppressed; a stronghold in times of trouble ... Oh, that salvation for Israel would come out of Zion! When the Lord restores the fortunes of his people, let Jacob rejoice and Israel be glad!"

See also, Psalm 91:7; Psalm 142:5; 2 Samuel 22:3.)

Prayer

Thank you, my Lord and Master for the reassurance that you are my refuge and strength. I appreciate you for being there for me in every situation. I worship you almighty God! Amen.

PRESERVE ME

Prepare me to

Reach souls who will choose

Eternal life that comes through

Salvation in Jesus Christ,

Emmanuel, who is always ready to

Redeem the lost because of His

Vicarious sacrifice and

Efficacious love and grace.

Psalm 32:7 (NIV) states, "You are my hiding place; you will protect me from trouble and surround me with songs of deliverance."

(See also, Psalm 121:7–8; Luke 17:32; 2 Timothy 4:18.)

<u>Prayer</u>
Father God, certainly you preserve those who live for you and call upon your name, in honor and praise to you. Therefore, I bless your name for your preserving power in the midst of trouble. Amen.

WEEK 6

PROSPERITY

Peace and righteousness have kissed each other for the

Redeemed of the Lord to reside in the kingdom of God in

Obedience to the Lover of their soul, who freely gives them

Salvation and enables them to walk in the spirit where they enjoy

Peace that passes all human understanding.

Experiencing nothing broken or missing and being in a state of wholeness

Rejuvenates the beloved of God as they

Imitate Christ and seek to maintain a personal relationship with Him. They redeem the

Time and seize the opportunity to do God's will as they

Yield to the path of their destiny in Him.

Joshua 1:8 (NIV) states, "Do not let this Book of the Law depart from your mouth; meditate on it day and night, so that you may be careful to do everything written in it. Then you will be prosperous and successful."

(See also, 3 John 2.)

Prayer

My Lord and King, it is your will for me to prosper but, I am incomplete without you making prosperity a reality in my life as I meditate on your precepts. Therefore, since you are the creator of all resources, both tangible and intangible, I submit to your Lordship, all areas of my life, in order to live a disciplined lifestyle. Thank you very much for your grace and mercy. Thank you for peace that surpasses understanding. Help me to make my life a sermon of prosperity that reflects your character, In Jesus' name. Amen!

WHAT IS MEEKNESS?

Meekness is a virtue that emanates from the character of Christ.
Meekness is strength under control.
Meekness is putting a bridle on your tongue when you know the truth is evident.
Meekness is reflected in your walk, not your talk.
Meekness is service with a smile even when you are emotionally abused, because you know that God is your vindicator.
Meekness is allowing your gifts to make room for you, because your promotion comes from God.
Meekness is being submissive to God's will as you live a lifestyle of humility and patience.

Mighty God causing me to submit to His authority, subsequently

Enhancing His attributes internally and externally

Even tempered, but solid as a rock.

Kindness in word and deed.

Nobility among crowds, to express the

Excellence of King Jesus to bring

Salvation and

Spiritual revelation to those who seek Him for His glory and honor.

1 Timothy 6:6-11 (NIV) states, "But godliness with contentment is great gain. For we brought nothing into the world, and we can take nothing out of it. But if we have food and clothing, we will be content with that. People who want to get rich fall into temptation and a trap and into many foolish and harmful desires that plunge men into ruin and destruction. For the love of money is the root of all kinds of evil. Some people, eager for money, have wandered

from the faith and pierced themselves with many griefs. But you, man of God, flee from all this, and pursue righteousness, godliness, faith, love, endurance and gentleness."

Prayer

God, you are the great Ruler of my life. Teach me to be like Jesus, who did not open His mouth during periods of severe humiliation on my behalf. I will honor you with my life daily. In Jesus' name. Amen.

WEEK 7

MEEKNESS IS

Meekness is one of the nine fruits of the spirit.
Meekness personifies Jesus because
He was led as a Lamb to the slaughter.
They spat upon Him and beat Him.
They also called Him ugly names, and
He did not respond or react.

Meekness is knowing that you are falsely
Accused and misjudged, called degrading and
Ungodly names and not react
With similar accusations, misjudging
And speaking words that damage the soul and the heart.

Meekness is knowing that you are not perfect,
Because all have sinned and come short of the glory of God.
Therefore, you do not crucify the individual who wronged you
Because you know that, greater is He that is in you
Than the enemy who is using people as instruments.

Meekness is yielding your right when you know
That it would be a disaster if you did not.
Meekness is seeking peace and pursuing it
In order to protect others from themselves,
Because they are vulnerable.

Meekness is knowing the truth and not
Defending yourself in the face of destructive criticisms
And false accusations because you know that,
God is your Vindicator.

Meekness is knowing that you are human,
But sealed with the assurance that your life is hid with Christ in God.
Therefore, unforgiveness, revenge and bitterness
Cannot reside in your heart, spirit and body
Because you are the temple of the Holy Ghost.

Meekness comes from love,
Godly love----agape, unconditional love.
So, begin to use meekness as a weapon, a "love" weapon,
To kill and to overcome the strategies of the enemy,
As he uses and manipulates people to destroy
Your self-worth and motivation.

Meekness is rooted in the core of your being,
Although your eyes well up with tears,
And the tears roll down your cheeks,
You are unmovable, unshakeable and always abounding in the truth.

Matthew 5:5(NIV) States, "Blessed are the meek for they will inherit the earth."

(See also, Galatians 5:23; Ephesians 4:1-4; 1 Timothy 6:11.)

Prayer

God, you are Lord of my life. I love you very much for providing the way to salvation, reconciliation and redemption through Jesus, your son. Cause me this day and always to exercise your unconditional love to everyone, irrespective of the circumstances. In Jesus' name. Amen.

PRAY

Press and push

Relentlessly after and toward the

All-knowing, all-powerful and awesome

Yahweh and surrender yourself to Him.

Psalm 27: 4, 8 (NIV) "One thing I ask of the LORD, this is what I seek: that I may dwell in the house of the LORD all the days of my life, to gaze upon the beauty of the LORD and to seek him in his temple. My heart says of you, "Seek his face!" Your face, LORD, I will seek."

Philippians 3:14 (NIV) "I press on toward the goal to win the prize for which God has called me heavenward in Christ Jesus."

(See also, Deuteronomy 4:29; Job 8:5; Mark 3:10; Luke 16:16.)

Persisting in thanksgiving, praise and worship will bring

Revival which causes us to experience
    an awakening to God's will for our lives and the

Assurance that God is concerned
    about every detail of our lives.

Yielding brings rest from our labor of
    trying to do what God alone can do.

1 Thessalonians 5:17–18 (NIV) states, "Pray continually, give thanks in all circumstances, for this is God's will for you in Christ Jesus."

(See also, James 5:14–15; Philippians 4:6; 1 Corinthians 2:2.)

<u>Prayer</u>

Father God in the name of Jesus, I thank you that you are concerned about every detail of my life. There is nothing hidden from you, that you have not seen. Therefore Lord, I bless your name and rely on you completely because you have every concern and issue in your charge. Thank you very much for ordering my steps. Amen!

WEEK 8

LIVING A LIFESTYLE OF PRAISE

Praise your way to victory with
The alphabet of praise.

A Alpha (Beginning), Author and Finisher of our faith, age to age you are the same, All-in-All, All-Powerful.

B Beautiful Rose of Sharon, Bright Morning Star, Balm of Gilead, Babe of Bethlehem, Burden Bearer, Bread of Life

C Compassionate One, Complete and Comforting One, Closer than a brother/sister/spouse/child, Conquering Lion of Judah, Counselor

D Daystar, Daily Bread, Daniel's Deliverer

E Everlasting Father, Emmanuel, Ever-Present, El Shaddai, Elohim, Everything to me, Excellent God.

F Faithful One, Father of fathers, Food when I'm hungry, Forgiver of sins, Friend indeed and in need, Father to the fatherless.

G God of gods, Gracious One, Glorious God, Great God, Giver of Life, Great Physician

H Hallelujah to your name, Holiest of all, Hosanna to the Highest, Hezekiah's God, Health insurance, Healer of my body.

I Indwelling in the believers to bring power, I am that I am.

J   Jehovah Jireh, Jehovah Shalom, Jehovah Rapha, Jehovah-Nissi, Justifier, Judah's Lion.

K   Kings of Kings, kindest of all

L   Lords of lords, Lover of my soul, living water, light of the world

M   Most Holy, Mighty One of Israel, Mighty God, More than enough, Merciful God, Miraculous God.

N   Never-failing One, Noblest of all.

O   Omnipotent, Omniscient, Overcomer, Overflowing-Joy, Omega.

P   Potter of my life, Precious Stone that Daniel saw rolling into Babylon, Precious Cornerstone of my life, Pleasures for evermore.

Q   Quality to the cheap, Quencher of thirsty souls.

R   Resurrected One, Risen with healing in His wings, Restorer of my soul, Redeemer, Rose of Sharon

S   Savior of my soul, Salvation to the lost, Spirit and Life, Supplier of my needs, Source of my life, Strength of my life, Strong-Tower.

T   Teacher, Truth, Trusted-One.

U   Union of God, the Father, Son, and Holy Spirit, Unconditional Love.

V   Victorious One, Vicarious Savior, Vine.

W   Water when I'm thirsty, Wheel in the middle of the wheel, Way-Maker, Worthiest of all.

X X-ray of the supernatural that sees within the human heart, soul and spirit, motives and intentions

Y Yesterday, Today, and Forever, Yoke Destroyer

Z Zeal-Giver.

Psalm 34:1(NIV) states, "I will extol the Lord at all times; his praise will always be on my lips. My soul will boast in the lord; let the afflicted hear and rejoice. Glorify the Lord with me; let us exalt his name together. I sought the Lord, and he answered me; he delivered me from all fears. Those who look to him are radiant; their faces are never covered with shame."

(See also, Psalm 50:23, 65:1, 71:6, 14, 119:164.)

Prayer
Hallelujah to the Lamb of God! There is none to compare with you! I shall flow with praise for you daily so that my life is enveloped with the sacrifices of praise. Help me to sing praises to you when the days are filled with negativity and disappointments, because hope arise in the praises to you. Amen.

LIGHT

Lord of my life

Illuminate me with your presence so that

Goodness and Mercy which follow me, shall

Help me to bring to others

Truth, and light that personify you.

Psalm 18: 28 (KJV) states, "For thou wilt light my candle: the Lord my God will enlighten my darkness."

Psalm 36:9 (NIV) states, "For with you is the fountain of life; for in your light we see Light."

Psalm 67:1 (NIV) states, "May God be gracious to us and make His face shine upon us."

Psalm 119:105 (NIV) states, "Thy Word is a lamp for my feet and a light for my path.

Matt 5:14–16 (NIV) states, "You are the light of the world. A city on a hill cannot be hidden. Neither do people light a lamp and put it under a bowl. Instead they put it on a stand, and it gives light to everyone in the house."

Prayer

Dearest Father, my deepest desire is to let my light shine for you because my soul is the candle of the Lord. Thank you for sending Jesus, for bringing the light of life to extinguish the darkness in the soul of lost humanity. I shall make the choice to keep my light brightly burning, through Jesus. Amen.

Week 9

Hallelujah Anyhow

When the way seems dark and dreary
And it's like there's no silver lining
Behind the thick, dark clouds,
Don't give up, say hallelujah anyhow!

When toils and persecution come your way
And the battle seems hard to fight,
Fight on and conquer, it's Hallelujah anyhow!

When the hosts of hell assail and
Fear presents itself,
Have faith and say, it's Halleujah anyhow!

When the world seems upside down,
Like it's about to fall into nothingness
Say, 'Rock of ages hide thou me' and
Hallelujah anyhow!

When the finances dry up,
A dime you cannot find,
Hold onto the Provider and say,
Hallelujah anyhow!

When your life's goals are not achieved and
Everything seems to fail
Relax in the arms of the One who holds the future
And say, hallelujah anyhow!

When your work here seems unappreciated
And there is no reward from man,
Keep heart and look to the Rewarder of your faith

And say, hallelujah anyhow!

When discouragement and grievances
Try to knock you down and
It seems like the race is incomplete
Reach out to Jesus and say, hallelujah anyhow!
When old age creeps in and the sight gets dim,
Stay close to the Giver of Life,
He'll give you eternal life.
Then you will say, hallelujah anyhow!

When the chilly hands of death you feel
Take you to your rest
Be ready and say, hallelujah anyhow!

Isaiah 43:2 (NIV) states, "When you pass through the water, I will be with you; and when you pass through the rivers, they will not sweep over you. When you walk through the fire you will not be burned; the flames will not set you ablaze."

Prayer

Father God, I praise and thank you for the peace you give in the storms. Surely, you are the Rewarder of those who diligently seek you. This is the day that you have made; I shall rejoice and be glad in it. Amen.

Declaration of God's Elect Lady

I am an elect lady whom God loves.
He has called me to his grace, mercy and peace,
Therefore, I shall have His favor,
I shall be blessed in my going out and my coming in.

God shall cause people to give me favor in everything I do.
If a door is closed, it's God who ordained it so
That a bigger door is opened for
Greater favor and greater blessings.

Because I am the elect of God,
My husband shall **seek the peace of God**
And he shall have favor.
He shall **see the way, work the word of God**
And **walk in the anointing of God.**

Since I am the elect of God, everyone whose life I touch,
Shall never be the same as before I touched them.
This elect lady shall transmit **truth, hope** and **life**
So that when people see me, they'll see Jesus
Illuminating and radiating thru' my **love** for them.

The elect of God puts on
Tender-mercies, meekness, humility,
Kindness, longsuffering, forgiving one another
and bearing one another's burdens.

The elect lady is predestined to walk
In the will of God and to live
The sermon of God's Love.

2 John 1:1–3a (NIV) states, "To the chosen lady and her children, whom I love in the truth and not I only, but also all who know the truth because of the truth, which lives in us and will be with us forever: Grace, mercy and peace from God the Father."

(See also, Colossians 3:12–13.)

<u>Prayer</u>
Bless the Lord O my soul and all that is within me! Bless His holy name. Lord you are great! I appreciate you for your unconditional and unfailing love. Teach me and cause me to walk in your word so that my life is a constant sermon that will draw others to you by the work of your Holy Spirit. Amen.

WEEK 10

FORGIVENESS IS

The act of excusing someone for a fault or offense
The act of renouncing resentment against someone.

When you choose to forgive, you:

    Unlock the handcuff of hell or the prison of sin.
    Open the heart for God to bless you.
    Open the doors of success.
    Choose to receive the grace of God.
    Choose to walk in good health.
    Choose to be used by God as His instrument.

Forgive the
Offender by
Reaching into the heart of
God for His grace and
Infinite mercy. Think of the
Vicarious sacrifice of Jesus and His
Eternal existence and
Never-failing love. Then
Enter a new arena of
Success and
Security that come with choosing to forgive.

Fall

On your knees.

Repent before your

God and show Him the

Inside of your heart that's filled with

Vexation and pain that seem like

Eternity and

Not getting any better.

Enter His gates with thanksgiving.

Shout loud His goodness and mercy.

Sing unto Him a new song for your deliverance.

Colossians 1:14; (NIV) states," In whom we have redemption, the forgiveness of sins."

(See also, Mark 11:25; Psalm 86:5; Acts 13:38, 26:18; Ephesians 1:7.)

Prayer

Heavenly Father, please grant me the heart of your son Jesus, so I will find it easy to forgive my offenders and accusers. Because it's in forgiving that I receive forgiveness from you. I have no choice but to lay the burden of negative emotions at the altar. So, I give you my life. Today and always, I shall rejoice in your goodness. In the mighty name of Jesus. Amen

GRACE

God's gift of beauty, charm, divine love and mercy that
Reach to those who believe and seek after God for
All His attributes to bring a
Change from within, resulting in an outward manifestation of
Everlasting joy and peace.

Grace is the empowering presence of God manifested in
Goodwill that comes from
Resting in God, while being
Active disciples with
Charm and
Everlasting joy.

Ephesians 2:4–5, 7–8 (NIV) states, "But because of his great love for us, God, who is rich in mercy, made us alive with Christ even when we were dead in transgressions—it is by grace you have been saved … in order that in the coming ages he might show the incomparable riches of his grace, expressed in his kindness to us in Christ Jesus. For it is by grace you have been saved, through—faith and this not from yourselves, it is the gift of God."

See also, Romans 5:2; 1Corinthians 15:10; 2 Corinthians 6:1–2; Ephesians 8:9; 2 Corinthians 12:9.)

Prayer

O God, thanks for your grace, it is an awesome gift. It could only be you, who has showered us with such indescribable virtue that goes beyond human understanding. Therefore Lord, my desire is to make a positive difference in my community for your honor and glory. Amen.

WEEK 11

CHANGE

Change is the product of seeing oneself and actively growing to be like Jesus by putting on the righteousness of God.

Change must be substantive and sustaining.

Consecration of all members of the body
    to bring them into subjection to the

Holiness of God and an

Awareness of His presence, which results in

Newness of mind for the believers
    and transitioning them from

Glory to glory into

Eternity with everlasting joy.

Colossians 2:6 (NIV) states, "So then, just as you received Christ Jesus as Lord, continue to live in Him, rooted and built up in Him, strengthened in the faith as you were taught and overflowing with thankfulness."

(See also, 2 Corinthians 3:18.)

Prayer

Redeeming Lord, thank you for your transforming power through your son Jesus. It is impossible for me to fathom the miracle that comes with the born again experience. So, I accept your love because it is substantive and sustaining. Your love causes me to think of you on a daily, so others will be moved to accept Jesus as Lord of their life. Amen!

C͟o͟n͟s͟e͟c͟r͟a͟t͟e͟ Y͟o͟u͟r͟ M͟e͟m͟b͟e͟r͟s͟

Place yourself in the hands of God,
Eradicate corrupt and selfish thoughts
Then produce words of wisdom for the
Inspiration and edification of souls.

Repair your vision to be prepared for what is coming next
Then as a result no one will perish.
Listen to God for His command and guidance
Before making a leap for your own goals.

Sanctify your hands to do what the Lord wants you do.
Follow in the footsteps of the Savior, you'll never go wrong.
He'll lead you always in the paths of righteousness.
Cry out and say, "Let me lose myself and find it Lord in thee."

As you walk, seek peace and pursue it,
Because Jesus said blessed are the peacemakers,
They shall be called the children of God.
Rest in the lover of your soul and
Your sleep shall be sweet.

Romans 12:1–3 (NIV) states, "Therefore, I urge you, brothers, in view of God's mercy, to offer your bodies as living sacrifices, holy and pleasing to God—this is your spiritual act of worship. Do not conform any longer to the pattern of this world, but be transformed by the renewing of your mind. Then you will be able to test and prove what God's will is—His good, pleasing and perfect will.

For by the grace given me I say to every one of you: Do not think of yourself more highly than you ought, but rather think of yourself with sober judgment, in accordance with the measure of faith God has given you. "

(See also, 1 Thessalonians 5:23, Psalm 34:14; Matthew 5:9, 13–16.)

Prayer

Father God, you are worthy of my praise and adoration, so I lift my hands and my voice to worship you. It is such a wonderful and satisfying experience to know you Lord, because in you, there is ultimate peace and joy. Please keep me in the shadow of your wings so that I will be set apart for your use and your glory. Amen!

WEEK 12

I Am God's Child

I am the Righteousness of God — 2 Corinthians 5:21

My ears shall hear only what God wants me to hear.
  Psalm 51:8; 1 John 4:6

My eyes shall see only what God sees.
  Psalm 32:8; Luke 2:30; 1 John 2:16; Proverbs 22:9

My feet shall go only where God wants me to go to seek peace and pursue it.
  Isaiah 52:7; Romans 10:15.

My hands shall only do what God wants them to do because they are an extension of His hands.
  Colossians 3:17

My heart—I shall guard my heart, my soul, and my spirit by refusing to accept negativism and participating in gossip.
  Matthew 12:34a–37; Mark 15:17–20a; Philippians 4:8–9

My mind shall be renewed daily by the word of God and I refuse to allow the devil to use my mind as a playing field.
  Ephesians 4:22–27; Psalm 119:1; Proverbs 6:20–23

My mouth shall speak success and not failure, only life and not death.
  Colossians 3:8–10

1 Corinthians 6:19–20 (NIV) states, "Do you not know that your body is a temple of the Holy Spirit, who is in you, whom you have

received from God? You are not your own; you were bought at a price. Therefore. honor God with your body."

(See also, 2 Corinthians 5:21.)

Prayer

Creator of my life, you predestined me to serve you and to bring honor and praise to your name. Therefore, I present my whole being to you, so that I will be effective In reaching others with the gospel of Jesus. Thank you very much for your preservation. Amen.

ANGER

A feeling of extreme wrath, hostility, indignation or exasperation.

> God's wrath is different from man's wrath.
> God's anger is a holy wrath against sin.
> Genesis 30:2; Exodus 4:14, 32:22; Psalm 27:9–11

Man's wrath: a manifestation of anger
- Violent
- Resentful anger
- Rage

Allowing

Negative vibes and

Garbage to

Enter your spirit and

Rush you into rage.

Proverbs 16:32 (NIV) states, "He that is slow to anger is better than the mighty, and rules his spirit is better than he that taketh a city."

James 1:19 (NIV) states, "My beloved brethren let every man be
---- swift to hear
---- slow to speak
---- slow to wrath."

Prayer
My Lord and master, I thank you that each day when I wake up, you cause me not to allow negative vibes and garbage of circumstances and situations enter my spirit and rush me into rage. I take a stand against the enemy of my soul—the devil. I will let Jesus reign in all areas of life. Amen.

WEEK 13

SHOW ME AN ANGRY PERSON

Show me an angry person
And you will see an internally
Bruised and wounded individual
Who fails to forgive the person who commits the offense.

Show me an angry person
And you will see an individual who
Is very limited with mercy and who keeps
Pointing fingers at others.

Show me an angry person
And you will see a soul dying
From within and holding on to the past
Of good and evil and is refusing to surrender
Those things that prevent progress toward destiny with God.

Show me an angry person
And you will see behind the facade a person who expresses
Love for the Lord and yearns to do the will of God
But refuses to love the ones who
committed the offense

Show me an angry person
And you will see behind the heart of stone
A lump of flesh that cries out to God
When there is no other way out
And the struggle to do right becomes more challenging.

Show me an angry person
And you will see a perfectionist at heart
Who expects everyone to be without fault,

But finds it hard to believe that when the moment of truth arises,
Only God is perfect and as humans we must strive
For the fruits of the spirit—temperance, peace, and long-suffering.

Show me an angry person
And you will see displacement of trust
Confidence in man rather than God who is the
Author and Finisher of our faith.

Show me an angry person
And you will see shattered hopes and dreams that have not been
Materialized or come to pass, because that
Individual allows procrastination and fear to steal
Every opportunity that time allows.

Show me an angry person
And you will see an individual who
Thinks he controls everything, then
When others cause circumstances to change
He exhibits a temper tantrum and loses control
Of his spirit and emotions,
Like a city without walls.

Very soon when the angry person who loves God
Realizes that anger rests in the bosom of fools
And that the mighty is temperate in all things.
With humility, that person will seek for
Intimacy in his relationship
With a merciful and loving God
Who is slow to anger, shall
Provide a way to help him
Grow in favor with God and man.

Proverbs 29:11 (NIV) states, "A fool gives full vent to his anger but a wise man keeps himself under control."

(See also, Ecclesiastes 7:9)

Prayer
Lord, today I surrender my negative emotions to you because my thoughts or actions that allow me to violate my relationship with you, create unrest within my innermost being and the Holy Spirit who lives in me is grieved. So, I praise you and thank you that I walk in discipline—resting assured that you are in total control of my life. In Jesus' name I give you praise and thanks for your love. Amen.

EMOTIONAL ABUSE IS NOT OF GOD

Emotional abuse is a long sharp sword that is driven very deep within the human soul. Without God's intervention, it will take a lifetime to heal—if ever—because those memories do not leave like people do. We are the masterpiece of God's creation. Therefore, no-one has the right to even attempt to undermine God. The enemy, however, is divisive and sometimes uses a loved one as an instrument to strip you of healthy self-esteem, noteworthiness and sense of value. Satan allows that loved one to cut through to the core of your God-given soul. That is not of God.

Emotional abuse is a weapon that, slowly and meticulously slices the emotions of the inner man, millimeter by millimeter and inch by inch. Satan uses the greedy and controlling spirit in that instrument to misuse time and mental energy to create and inflate lies and illusions of your intentions for them to appear real. Then the victim experiences feelings of defenselessness, emptiness and humiliation. That is not of God.

When the abuser doesn't feel like he's doing an effective job because there is no reaction or tears rolling down the cheeks of his victim, he recalls historical events and paints an enormously twisted picture with words such as, "See, I can't trust you. There you go again, being disrespectful to me." This infliction is manipulated by Satan, the enemy of our souls, who constantly uses the abuser as his instrument to become fixated on unfulfilled expectations with anger and a judgmental spirit.

The convincing pseudo mind-reader becomes irate that the victim never dares to speak. Oh, what mood swings, no one knows which direction the handle may fly off or which crack it may get stuck and for how long. That is not of God.

With the spirit of manipulation and self-centeredness, there is a constant repetition of, "If you don't do what I say and listen to me, God will give me someone else who will listen and do what I say.

God will destroy anything that is a stumbling block to me." The victim then continues to struggle with being focused on God's will. Then the tantalizing question keeps popping up, "Will I ever do anything right?" That is not of God.

God, the Holy Spirit is our helper during unsettling and challenging times, especially when emotional abuse becomes the order of the hour, day, week, month or years. God has not called or predestined any of His human creation to be the giver or receiver of emotional abuse. That is not of God.

Look to the center of your joy, and the lover of your soul, Jesus, because He is your vindicator. He made you a winner and more than a conqueror. He will rush strength to you in moments when you forfeit your rights for the common good.

1 Peter 2:9 (NIV) states, "But you are a chosen people, a royal priesthood, a holy nation, a people belonging to God, that you may declare the praises of him who called you out of darkness into his wonderful light."

(Also see, Ephesians 1:2–6; Galatians 5:26; Matthew 12:34–37; Malachi 4:1–6.)

Prayer

Dearest Lord Jesus, I love and appreciate you for being my great hiding place. There is none like you. You are the center of my joy and the wind beneath my wings. Thank you very much for being my strength and my fortress. Father, I present to you all those individuals who are experiencing emotional hurts that you will caress them with your loving arms. Please let them accept the healing of those internal bruises and scars because you specialize in making them whole through and through. I praise you, in Jesus' name. Amen.

What Will You Do with this Man, Jesus?

Will you accept Him or reject Him?

The man, Jesus, who was with God from the beginning of creation.
Will you accept or reject Him?
The man who turned water into wine
In Cana of Galilee at the wedding.
The man, Christ Jesus, who came to earth as the Messiah to lost humanity.
A gift that no earthly father would have given to mankind.
What will you do with Him?
Will you accept or reject Him?

The man "Christ Jesus is the Living Water.
He invites everyone to drink of the water that He provides
Because they shall never thirst again. His living water is
as a well of water springing up into everlasting life.
He beckons to the thirsty souls to come and drink from him.
What will you do with this Jesus?
Will you accept or reject Him?

What will you do with the great physician, the man, Jesus?
He healed the man who was infirmed and crippled for thirty-eight years.
He felt virtue left Him when the woman with the blood disease touched Him.
She received a miraculous change in her body through her faith in Jesus.
His will for his children is to be prosperous in health.
Will you accept or reject this man, Jesus, He cares for you.

The man, Christ Jesus, who came down from heaven
As the bread of God and gives life to the world,
Will you accept or reject Him?
The bread of Life who invites all who

Are hungry to come and eat and live forever.
And again, the question is, what will you do with this man Jesus?
Will you accept or reject him?

Christ the forgiving and merciful one who asked the woman
Caught in the act of adultery, for the accusers who
Attempted to condemn her, there were none present.
By His grace and love, He assured her that He did not condemn her
And that He freed her from all wrongdoing and introduced
Her to a new lifestyle.

So, then what will you do with the light of the world
Who declares that anyone who follows Him shall not walk in darkness,
But shall have the light of life.
The question remains, what will you do with this Jesus?
Will you accept or reject Him?

Yes, that same man whom Isaiah spoke about,
Was wounded for our transgressions,
Bruised for our infirmities.
The chastisement of our peace was upon him,
And with His stripes we are healed.
O what love for humanity this man, Jesus, has.
He poured out His soul unto death.

He was numbered with the transgressors
So, the irresistible question still resounds,
What will you do with this man, Jesus, the Anointed one?
He made a way of escape for lost souls from
The terrible judgment of God's wrath.
Will you accept Him? Or will you reject Him?
The man, Christ Jesus.

1Timothy 2:5 (NIV) states, "For there is one God and one mediator between God and men, the man Jesus Christ."

(See also, Romans 3:29; Hebrews 8:6; John 1–15.)

<u>Prayer</u>

My dear Father in heaven, I thank you for sending Jesus to pay the price for my sin and for giving up the splendor of heaven in order to experience the earthly realm and be able to relate and understand human emotions. O what unconditional love and incomparable sacrifice. I love you, and I praise and adore you because you first loved me.

I have no choice but to accept Jesus in my life and to cherish this awesome relationship. Help me daily to let Jesus shine through me to others who will accept Him as Lord of their lives. In Jesus' name. Amen

WEEK 14

WAIT

Wait patiently for that

Appointed time set for everything
    God has ordained for us to do.

Into His hands we
    unreservedly and without hesitation,

Turn every situation over to Him,
    because He is in control.

Waiting is enveloped in time.
Time is continuous and alive.
Therefore, God is time manifested
In Jesus, who is the same
Yesterday, today and forever.

Time is an unexplainable and unfathomable
Resource given to man by God.
Man has no choice but to live and be active
one day at a time and to watch the events
of each day themselves timely unfold
according to God's will.

Therefore, we must listen to God,
long for Him and love Him as
He gently leads us into our destiny with Him.

Psalm 25:5 (NIV) states, "Guide me in your truth and teach me, for you are God my Savior, and my hope is in you all day long."

(See also, Proverbs 20:22; Isaiah 8:17.)

<u>Prayer</u>
I love you Lord and praise you for whom you are. Certainly, my times are in your hands. Yes, Lord, sometimes waiting can be painful, but the rewards for waiting on your appointed time is sweet and fulfilling. Lord, teach me to wait for you. In Jesus' name. Amen.

THE LORD IS MY PROTECTION

Perfect Patriarch of generals has my life in His control.
  When life's overwhelming situations seem to overcome me,
  He provides a

Rugged mountain where I hide
  With His divine protection. He overshadows me
  with the evergreen branches on top of the mountain and breathes
  fresh inspiration in my innermost being.

Overpowering and over-ruling any destructive device of the enemy,
  my supernatural Commander holds me safely in the palm of
  His hands as a

Treasure. Like the jeweler, He strips away the undesirables,
  molds and shapes me as a special and precious gem
  that cannot be easily broken. Surely His presence

Encompasses me and no intruder can penetrate the perimeter of my
  surrounding. His wings of love spread wide and far to

Cover me like the eagle covers her eaglets so that no harm will
  come near.

Tower of divine refuge from my enemies, He is the only one that
  I look up to for His magnificence that brings absolute rest in
  my soul.

Illumination comes from Him because His glory outshines every
  light known to man.

Overwhelming victory is my song as it echoes from the depth of
  my soul with praises bellowing from by lips in honor of my
  great God who

Never fails to protect and keep me safe in His pavilion.

Psalm 18:1–3 (NIV) states, "I love you, O LORD, my strength, The LORD is my rock, my fortress and my deliverer; my God is my rock, in whom I take refuge. He is my shield and the horn of my salvation, my stronghold. I call to the LORD, who is worthy of praise, and I am saved from my enemies." (See also, Psalm 91:2.)

Prayer

You are great. You do miracles so great. So, Father God, I bless your name and honor you because you are my protection and my hiding place. Therefore, I have no fear.

Thank you. Amen.

THE GLORY OF THEM ALL

Look, look, the glories of God are everywhere.
We can see them in the apparent movements of
the sun, moon, clouds and the sea
with its colors of variegated hue.

The mountains so tall, are calling to come up higher.
The valleys oh so unique, which remind me of
the Psalm 23:4 "Even though I walk through the valley
of the shadow of death, I'll fear no evil."
Oh, how marvelous it is to walk in the steps of the Savior as
we walk on the beautiful green grass.

God is a God of variety.
That silver moonlight and the stars which brighten
the world at night in the absence of the golden sun.
My God, He's such a beautiful God.
Look at the colorful flowers with sweet smelling fragrances.

The chirping birds, making melodious sounds,
against the background of the whistling wind.
Just listen, please listen, oh so wonderful.
My God is so big, He has the universe in His hands.

I cannot, just cannot express
The wanders and the glories of God.
So, let us join hands and hearts together
and bask in the glory of them all.

Psalm 95:4–6 states, "In his hand are the depths of the earth and the mountain peaks belong to him. The sea is his, for he made it, and his hands form the dry land. Come, let us bow down in worship let us kneel before the Lord our maker."

(See also, Genesis 1:1–31.)

Prayer

Glorious are you God. The whole earth is filled with your glory. So, I worship you Almighty God with my whole being. I appreciate you for who you are—the Creator of the universe, the Giver of life and love.

Please help me daily, to reflect on your never-failing love and glory. Let me never take for granted the beautiful gifts that you have given me. Thank you, Lord. In the strong name of Jesus. Amen.

WEEK 15

STEWARDSHIP

Sold out to the

Techniques of

Exercising our spiritual abilities with God's wondrous

Works because He has made us

Accountable to Him and

Responsible for our actions, His resources and

Dauntless gifts.

Starting the day with

Him will

Inspire us to

Push forward in order to succeed daily.

Ephesians 1:17–18 (NIV) states, "I keep asking that the God of our Lord Jesus Christ, the glorious Father, may give you the Spirit of wisdom and revelation, so that you may know him better. I pray also that the eyes of your heart may be enlightened in order that you may know the hope to which he has called you, the riches of his glorious inheritance in the saints."

(See also, Romans 12:1–2.)

Prayer

Father God, in the name of Jesus I come to you today with an open heart and mind, appreciating you for the resources you have made available to me. You are my Jehovah Jireh—my provider. O what an awesome God you are. Teach me to implement your stewardship principles in all areas of my life. I worship you with my whole being and will not cease to praise you. Amen.

Satisfaction

Storing up treasures in heaven, where moth nor rust doth not corrupt,

Activates an interest-bearing account in the eternal bank of heaven.

Trusting God that all our needs are met as we live a lifestyle of stewardship with God given resources,

Initiating an intimate relationship with our Master who guarantees

Stability and strength during life's challenges.

Following consistently his precepts and leadership

Allows us to be more than conquerors because he loves us.

Committing our members to him unreservedly daily, results in

Total submission to God,

Irrespective of intervening variables and

Oppositions that present themselves from unexpected sources, let us

Never lose sight of the passion that God placed in us for His honor and glory.

Matthew 6:19–34(NIV) states, "Do not store up for yourselves treasures on earth, where moth and rust destroy, and where thieves break in and steal. But store up for yourselves, treasures in heaven, where moth and rust do not destroy, and where thieves do not break in and steal. For where your treasure is, there your heart will be also.

"The eye is the lamp of the body. If your eyes are good, your whole body will be full of light. But if your eyes are bad, your whole body will be full of darkness. If then the light within you is darkness, how great is that darkness!

"No one can serve two masters. Either he will hate the one and love the other, or he will be devoted to the one and despise the other. You cannot serve both God and Money.

"Therefore, I tell you, do not worry about your life, what you will eat or drink; or about your body, what you will wear. Is not life more important than food, and the body more important than clothes? Look at the birds of the air; they do not sow or reap or store away in barns, and yet your heavenly Father feeds them. Are you not much more valuable than they? Matthew 6:19-34 Can any of you by worrying can add a single hour to his life?

"And why do you worry about clothes? See how the lilies of the field grow. They do not labor or spin. Yet I tell you that not even Solomon in all his splendor was dressed like one of these. If that is how God clothe the grass of the field, which is here today and tomorrow is thrown into the fire, will he not much more clothe you, O you of little faith? So do not worry, saying, 'What shall we eat?' or 'What shall we drink?' or 'What shall we wear?' For the pagans run after all these things, and your heavenly Father knows that you need them. But seek first his kingdom and his righteousness, and all these things will be given to you as well. Therefore, do not worry about tomorrow, for tomorrow will worry about itself. Each day has enough trouble of its own."

Prayer
O Lord my God, excellent is Your name and all our precepts. I rest in the knowledge that You satisfy me completely because I made the decision to follow Your commandments to the best of my ability. I know I am not perfect, but my desire is to seek you daily because it's in your presence I get satisfaction. Amen.

PEACE

Prince of peace give me
   that comfort and ease with

Everlasting tranquility that comes
   only from you, as the

Assurance that you are truly the

Conquering Lion of Judah
   who comes and

Extricate the lies of the enemy and vindicate
   your beloved one to a place of perfect rest
   because vengeance is yours.

John 14:27 (NIV) states, "Peace I leave with you; my peace I give you. I do not give to you as the world gives. Do not let your hearts be troubled and do not be afraid." (See also, Ephesians 2:14; 1 Peter 3:11; Romans 12:18–19; Colossians 3:15.)

Prayer

Lord God, I thank you that your Son came as both the Lion and the Lamb to give peace in the storm. Jesus, I appreciate you for your flexibility. Everything comes from you and in you there is no shadiness or darkness. There is such tranquility that comes with your light as it extinguishes darkness. I worship you almighty God! Hallelujah! Amen.

WEEK 16

<u>OBEDIENCE</u>

Obey the word of the Lord our God

Because it is meat to our bones and marrow.
  It breathes life into our spirit, soul and body.

Ever-living compass that never fails with perfect precision in giving

Direction for every situation in all areas of our lives.

Instilling the precepts of the spoken and written word in our heart and spirit we will be

Elevated to that place of rest and serenity with our Maker and Defender where

Nothing is broken or missing because the Prince of Peace sent the

Comforter who abides with us and ensures that

Everlasting joy, rests and remains with us for evermore.
  Choose obedience, the key to total peace.

James 1:25 (NIV) states, "But the man who looks intently into the perfect law that gives freedom, and continues to do this, not forgetting what he has heard, but doing it—he will be blessed in what he does." (See also, Hebrews 11:8; Acts 5:29.)

Prayer

Dear Lord, thank you for this day. It is so good to know you and to experience the peace and joy that emanate from such knowledge. Please help me today to follow your commands, because obedience is better than the sacrifice of material things to your cause or to any earthly program. Thank you for your strength through Jesus. Amen!

M-A-N

Mastery — God's masterpiece of creation. He was made to represent Him on earth. As the leader of his family, God made man accountable to Him for all provisions and made him a steward of them all.

Genesis 1:26 (NIV), "Then God said, 'Let us make man in our image, in our likeness, and let them rule over the fish of the sea and the birds of the air, over the livestock, over all the earth.'" (See also, Psalm 8:6.)

Anointing — When a man is submitted to his Maker, he receives the burden- removing and yoke-destroying power of God that sets him apart for God's sacred use.

Isaiah 10:27 (NIV), "In that day their burden will be lifted from your shoulders, their yoke from your neck; the yoke will be broken because you have grown so fat."

(See also, Ephesians 4:21–27; Ephesians 5:11; Colossians 1:12–14 21–23.)

Nobility — A mark of distinction bestowed upon man when he builds an intimate relationship with the Lover of His soul, Jesus.

Psalm 1:3 (NIV) states, "He is like a tree planted by streams of water, which yields its fruit in season and whose leaf does not wither. Whatever he does prospers."

(See also, Ecclesiastes 8:1; 1 Peter 2:9.)

Prayer
Father God, King of all kings, I thank you for all men who play significant roles in our lives. Lord, I ask that you ignite them with powerful illumination and understanding of who they are in You.

Cause them to see themselves as You see them. Revitalize and energize them to walk in discipline according to the call, You placed on their lives. Amen.

The Truth about Fatherhood

First created as a man to be faithful to his Maker, so he takes nothing for granted as he carries out his leadership responsibilities.

Always seeking to find pleasure in serving God and his family. With his shortcomings he

Tunes into the voice of the Giver of all good gifts to not be misled by worldly and ungodly influences and manipulation. The genuinely sensitive man

Heralds the truth and leads a life of integrity even when opportunities present themselves for violating these virtues.

Excellence is his pursuit because mediocrity is not an option, therefore, he never gives up but he is hopeful in all things and

Represents his family wherever he goes and is conscious of that ever-present *One* — his Lord God Almighty.

Proverbs 4:1–3 (NIV), "Listen, my sons, to a father's instruction; pay attention and gain understanding. I give you sound learning, so do not forsake my teaching. When I was a boy in my father's house, still tender, and an only child of my mother."

(See also, Psalm 22:4–5; Ephesians 6:4.)

<u>Prayer</u>
Heavenly Father God, in Jesus' name I come to You in awe of Your presence that is graceful, yet magnificent and electrifying. You are the greatest Father of all fathers. There is no imperfection in You. Thank you very much for setting an excellent example for all earthly fathers to follow. I lift up all fathers to You now. Give them the assurance that You are in control of every detail of their lives. You know their dreams, visions and goals. You will give them resources they need to accomplish them all. Cause them to understand such truth, teach them to submit their will to You and let Your will be done and Your kingdom come in their lives. Amen.

WEEK 17

MAN BORN OF WOMAN IS FULL OF TROUBLE

Temptations,

Rage and rude awakenings,

Oppression,

Uncleanness,

Battle at all stages,

Lifeless, lonely and lost,

Exhaustion! Enough is enough! Escape!

Nevertheless, Jesus, the second Adam,
Born of a woman, became
The sacrifice for our own sins
So that we shall inherit eternal life.
Because He lives, we shall live also
And have life more abundantly.

Psalm 14:1 states, "The fool says in his heart, 'There is no God.' They are corrupt, their deeds are vile; there is no one who does good."

(See also, Job 14:1-2; Psalm 27:5; Isaiah 33:2,6.)

Prayer

My God and Creator, I love and appreciate you very much for making a way of escape for us through Jesus, our Lord, who is the way, the truth and the life. It's through him that I have eternal life and I am victorious. So, allow me to teach others and direct them to the Way, the Truth and the Life. Amen!

Man—The Human Race

Born in sin, shaped in iniquity,
He's like a flower.
In the morning fresh and blooming,
In the evening withers away.

That physical, spiritual, emotional and social being
Seeks for popularity and superiority.
God's masterpiece of creation was made to serve the Lord.
Seeks to be on the mountaintop, but tends to be attracted
To all that glitters, as a result, finds himself in the lowest valley.

Man, with his self-pity and presumptuousness
Tries to compromise with sin and comforts
Himself with the thought, "God will understand".
He then comes to a crossroad.

Not knowing which way to choose
He falls on his knees when he sees
Himself insufficient, sinful and weak.
He then cries out, "God forgive me,
I've strayed far away from you,
Give me back my first love for you".

With a desperate heart for God he says,
"I want to follow you wherever you go.
Give me back my mountaintop experience
So that I may converse with you.
Apply your blood to my heart another time
So that I may receive strength from day to day".

Psalm 8:4-6 (NIV), "What is mankind that you are mindful of them, human beings that you care for them? You have made them a little lower than the angels and crowned them with honor. You made them rulers over the works of your hands; you put everything under their feet."

(See also, Psalm 5:1-4; Rom. 6:6.)

Prayer

Heavenly Father, thank you for giving me the opportunity to partake of another day here in the land of the living. You are altogether lovely. I praise you with my whole being. Teach me how to completely appreciate every gift that you have provided for me to enjoy every moment of the day. Amen.

Love Is

That constraining, restraining,
Maintaining and sustaining
Virtue is the fruit of the spirit.
Love, the most amazing force in life.
With its magnetic property
It draws two to become one,
And many to be in unity.

Love, God's gift—Jesus
Oh, so unfathomable
And past finding-out
Climbed Calvary's hill and died
On a rugged cross to redeem mankind.
Love is a paradox.
It can be our salvation or our undoing.
In its original and purest form, it is like life.
It must be carefully guarded and nurtured,
Lest it deteriorate and become
A curse instead of a blessing.

That magnetic force,
Which draws men to Christ
Develops a great affection within them
To address God as, "Loving Heavenly Father."
Honor and obedience are evident.
Genuine love desires to please the beloved one.
Then, there is joy to do the will of God.

Love is a tree
Which grows and grows
With its spreading branches
Of respect and tenderness.
Understanding and oneness,
Care and concern,
Honesty and humility,

> Straightforwardness and forgiveness,
> Protection and security
> True love, a tree
> With deep and eternal roots

1 Corinthians 13:8: (NIV) states, "Love never fails. But where there are prophesies, they will cease, where there are tongues, they will be stilled; where there is knowledge, it will pass away."

(See also John 3:16-18; Matthew 5:43-46).

Prayer

Father God, it is in the name of Your son Jesus I come to You, thanking You for Your goodness, grace and mercy. Your love is beyond measure and there is no limit to it. I desire that special love that only comes from You so that I can do exactly what You would like me to do for your honor and glory. Amen.

WEEK 18

LOVE NEVER FAILS

Love is like light that extinguishes darkness with the
Overwhelming presence of God. He offered Jesus as a
Vicarious sacrifice for mankind to have
Everlasting goodness, grace and glory.

Not puffed up, not easily provoked
Envies not.
Vanity is not evident.
Evil is not conceived or thought of.
Rejoices not in iniquity.

Fails not when other things cease to exist.
All things are endured and hopeful.
Its behavior is not unseemly and
Longsuffering is evident as she
Seeks not her own.

Proverbs 4:18 (NIV) states, "The path of the righteous is like the first gleam of dawn, shining ever brighter till the full light of day."

(See also, Matthew 5:14–16, 26:28; Psalm 16:11, 17:15; 1 Corinthians 1:30; Hebrews 9:28; John 1:14; 1 Corinthians 13:4–7; 2 Corinthians 3:18.)

Prayer

You are awesome and I adore You with the fruits of my lips and my whole life. You are my God and my everlasting portion. Thank you for Your unconditional love. Please help me to reach out to the unlovable, the unlovely, the unloved and the hard to love, so that Jesus will come alive through my love, that comes only from You. I praise You! In Jesus name. Amen.

BELOVED

We are His beloved because we are greatly loved by Him.

Bought with God's

Everlasting and unconditional

Love that was manifested through the

Overwhelming

Vicarious sacrifice of His only son Jesus, as

Evidenced by His

Death and resurrection for lost humanity.

Deuteronomy 33:12 (NIV) "Let the beloved of the Lord rest secure in him, for He shields him all day long, and the one the Lord loves rests between His shoulders."

(See also, Songs of Solomon 2:16; Daniel 9:23b; Romans 11:28–29.)

Prayer

You are worthy Lord God, to receive honor and glory because You are the ruler of my life. My heart and voice sing out with praise and love for You. There is no one like You. Thank you for choosing me as Your beloved through Jesus, my King of kings. Hallelujah. Amen.

LOVER

Light of the world, lifts me up above the shadows and the threats of the wicked and lets me

Overcome the trivial instigations and vindictiveness for me to live a

Victorious life to experience His prosperity. He then, with His

Everlasting grace and loving kindness

Redeemed me and made me His own.

Songs of Solomon 2:16 (NIV),"My lover is mine and I am his; he browses among the lilies."

Songs of Solomon 7:10 (NIV) "I belong to my lover and his desire is for me."

Prayer
O great lover of my soul, I love You because You first loved me. Let the light of Your love shine through me, so that others will be attracted to Your light and be led to You. Amen.

WEEK 19

Your Love Constrains and Restrains Me

Committed and consecrated to the cause of being

Overcomers in Christ Jesus, the author and finisher of our faith.

Never fainting nor failing to run the race of life with God, who makes us good

Stewards of

Talents, time and other

Resources including

All our finances according to the Master's

Instructions and inspiration by

Not bowing nor bending to the rudiments of this world's systems.

Your Love Restrains Me

Reach for the goal that leads to

Eternal destiny without

Stopping to react and yield to

Temptations, because it's in

Reacting that we are vulnerable to yielding. Therefore, we will not lose the

Assurance and confidence in our source, Jehovah Jireh, who

Instills within us that

Never-ending generosity and temperance which surpass human understanding.

2 Corinthians 5:13–15 (NIV) states, "If we are out of our mind, it is for the sake of God; if we are in our right mind, it is for you. For Christ's love compels us, because we are convinced that one died for all, and therefore all died. And he died for all, that those who live should no longer live for themselves but for him who died for them and was raised again."

(See also, Galatians 5: 22–26.)

Prayer
Mighty God, I bless Your name and honor You from the depth of my whole being. You are worthy to receive worship and adoration. Father, if it weren't for Your love that constrains and restrains me, I would be like a floating ball in a high wind. Therefore, I appreciate You very much for instilling Your love in me. Let me be a true witness of Your love—for Your honor and glory. Amen.

JESUS IS THE GATE

Jehovah saves those who believe
    that He is the Son of God who came to give

Eternal life, so when we repent and turn
    away from our sins, He will deliver and

Save our souls unto salvation and give victory over
    the enemy who comes to kill, steal and destroy.

Unreservedly and unconditionally, Emmanuel gives salvation
    and grace to those who enter through Him.

Stand firm and experience His goodness
    in the land of the living, since He is the
    God-given access to eternity.

John 3:16–17(NIV) states, "For God so loved the world that he gave his one and only Son, that whoever believes in Him shall not perish but have eternal life. For God did not send His Son into the world to condemn the world, but to save the world through Him." (See also, John 10:7–10, Hebrews 4:9–11, 14–16, 5:5–9.)

Prayer

Wonderful Lord and Savior, thank you for showing me the way to eternal life. Help me to encourage someone today and lead them to the gate, the God-given access to eternity, Jesus our Emmanuel. I praise your name. Amen.

I SHALL PREVAIL

When the battle gets hot and temptations soar high,
You are my defense because you brace me up with great grace
and flood my inner-being with your love and
your word that constrain and restrain me.

When the enemy uses my best friend
to exercise the tool of manipulation
in order to rob me of my God-given self-esteem,
I shall prevail because you are the
Source of my satisfaction and wellspring of life.

Yes, I shall prevail because you are my life, my joy, my all.
You preserve me in times of trouble
and you fight all my battles while
I sleep and while I am awake.

O precious general of my life,
I am in awe of the timeliness of your vindication.
Prevail I must, because I know that
when I am weak you make me strong.
How great and marvelous You are.

Job 22:25–28 (NIV), "Then the Almighty will be our gold, the choicest silver for you. Surely then you will delight in the Almighty and will lift up your face to God. You will pray to Him and he will hear you and you will fulfill your vows. What you decide on will be done, and light will shine on your ways."

(See also, Ephesians 1:3–7.)

Prayer

Bless the Lord O my soul and all that is within me. I praise You O my God because you are my victory. I win and I am more than a conqueror. Thank you for making me strong when I am weak. Hallelujah! Glory to your great name! Amen.

WEEK 20

JESUS, I'M IN NEED

Jesus, it's a crossroad. Which way should I go?
Should I go to the left side or right?
There is midnight all around Lord.
I've been through depression,
Distress, frustration, testing and tribulations.
I've had a broken heart, it has been
Mended and broken again. Master, what shall I do?

I've had many tears and sorrows,
Disappointments and failures.
I've wallowed in self-pity and have regretted it.
Father, I love you, and you know that I love you.
You know that I've always wanted to please you,
but somehow, I get weak, as a result I'm carried away.

Jesus, Holy One, I'm thirsty and parched,
Please fill me Lord, pump that well within me.
Yes Father, and let it flow high up into everlasting life.
I stop, think and visualize you, nailed to the cross of Calvary
For my redemption. You carried the heavy load
of my sins on your back.

Innocent one, it was no sin of your own but mine.
Thank you for wearing the crown of thorns
And drinking the bitter cup.
Thank you for interceding for me
But sweet Jesus, I'm still in need.
Father I'm waiting patiently for
Your still small voice and your tender touch of love.

Then Jesus emphatically and lovingly reminded me that,
He is the Way, the Truth and the Life.

And that He would lead me,
Reveal the truth and give me the light of life.
In John 11:25-26, His Reassurance was
Profound as He stated, "I am the Resurrection and the Life
He that believeth in me though
He were dead yet shall he live."

There is hope in His words stated in John 4:14
"I am the Living Water, this water that
I can give you, shall never run dry.
It's a well springing up into everlasting life."

With His compassionate voice,
Jesus implored me to believe and accept
His promises because in this world,
I would experience tribulations but He overcame,
which makes me more than a conqueror.

Matt 5:6 (NIV), "Blessed are those who hunger and thirst for righteousness, for they will be filled."

(See also, John 15: 1-26)

Prayer

Thank you, Lord. I love you, Lord. You are great, just great! You are wonderful! Thank you for the assurance that You are the omnipresent one. Here are my hands; lead me and guide me on the road to everlasting life. Amen.

Hope

Hope comes from our heavenly Father, who gives us

Heavenly mindset that lends itself for

Opportunities to choose the attitude of

Pushing and persisting to move from

Earthly temporal things to the eternal and celestial realm.

Roman 5:5 (NIV) states, "And hope does not disappoint us, because God has poured out his love into our hearts through the Holy Spirit, whom he has given us."

(See also, 1 Timothy 1:1; Titus 2:13; Hebrew 6:11.)

Prayer

Dear Lord God, I praise you because hope originates from You. You love and so with faith and hope we will not be ashamed because You will pull us through and make us victorious in the days to come. My hope is embedded in the rock of my salvation on whom I stand firm. Amen.

HUMILITY IS THE KEY

Hide and prepare yourself to be used as an instrument of His providence for the working out of His glorious purpose then God will

Unctionize us with His grace, power and glory as you focus on the

Message He has given you to live practically for others to see and strive toward an

Intimate relationship with Jesus.

Longing for a supernatural intervention will cause you to go

Into the secret closet where you will experience the dimensions of His presence through and through. There He burns away darkness of the soul to invoke purity as He prepares you and shapes you as His precious jewel so that you will be able to

Teach others of His unconditional love and great grace, which He gives to the humble, then you will find that

Your will is crucified for the cross of Jesus Christ and for the glory of God.

Philippians 2:5–11: (NIV®) states, "Your attitude should be the same as that of Christ Jesus: Who, being in very nature God, did not consider equality with God something to be grasped, but made himself nothing, taking the very nature of a servant, being made in human likeness. And being found in appearance as a man, he humbled himself and became obedient to death— even death on a cross! Therefore, God exalted him to the highest place and gave him the name that is above every name, that at the name of Jesus every knee should bow, in heaven and on earth and under the earth, and every tongue confess that Jesus Christ is Lord, to the glory of God the Father."

(See also, Proverbs 22:4; 1 Peter 5:5–7.)

<u>Prayer</u>

Father God, O how I yearn to be like Jesus. It certainly makes a difference when we submit to Your will, because it is in submitting that we learn the process of humility and in times of challenges of the soul and spirit. You give me great grace to overcome. I am very grateful to You and I praise You because You are a good God. Amen.

WEEK 21

HONOR

Heartfelt value and

Obedience that demonstrate the

Nobility of character, evidenced in the

Overcomer's life as he/she conforms to the image of Christ in order to

Respect and reverence the source of all good gifts and represent Him among nations.

James 1:17 (NIV) states, "Every good and perfect gift is from above, coming down from the Father of the heavenly lights, who does not change like shifting shadows."

(See also, 1 Peter 2:17; Romans 12:10; Exodus 20:12.)

Prayer

Dearest Lord and Father, it is in the name of Your beloved Son, Jesus, that I come into Your presence thanking You for Your grace and mercy that supports and sustains us daily. I honor You for who You are. Teach me how to truly give honor where it's due. Again, I praise and honor You for being my God! Amen.

Happiness Is

Health that is wholesome and
    healing in the mind, soul and body
    as we live a lifestyle of Godly stewardship of

All God-given resources.

Persisting with residing in the kingdom of God,
    which is not meat nor drink, but righteousness
    peace and joy in the Holy Ghost.

Prosperity, nothing lacking or broken

Intimacy with Christ which results in

No limitation to a lifestyle of worship to the King of kings
    and Lord of lords. He is the one who

Elevates those who

Surrender all earthly and carnal traditions and customs
    in order to be

Saturated in His presence and to reflect His glory.

Romans 14:17–19 (NIV) states, "For the kingdom of God is not a matter of eating and drinking, but of righteousness, peace and joy in the Holy Spirit, because anyone who serves Christ in this way is pleasing to God and approved by men. Let us therefore make every effort to do what leads to peace and to mutual edification."

(See also, Joshua 1:8; Psalm16:11; Proverbs 4:20–22; Colossians 2:6–11; 3 John 2.)

Prayer

Jehovah Jireh, You are our provider. You own the cattle on a thousand hills. You own everything in this world because You are the creator of them all. I bless your name! Teach us to rest in You and depend on You because all our needs are met by You. I have faith that once I live and move in You and depend on You as my source, happiness is always mine. Amen.

GUIDE ME

Guide me through the paths of righteousness
And let me feel the radiance of Your glory
Shining in my soul as the golden sun shines
Upon the world to bring about a new day.

Guide me through the valley
Of the shadow of death so that my soul will fear no evil.
Guide me through the testing, persecutions and tribulations,
So that I can lift the banner of victory high to encourage troubled souls.

Guide me when the restless waves are dashing
On the shores of life so that I can keep steady in the boat of assurance.
Guide me when it seems like my efforts are in vain,
and it's like there's no way out.

Guide me when the clouds are hanging low
And things seem to be totally out of sight
Hold me with Your hand of possibilities and opportunities,
And I will seize each moment.

Guide me when the enemy is soaring mad and wants me to see no success.
Help Lord, that by Your guidance I will reap life everlasting in
The celestial city that You have prepared for me.
There I shall worship you perpetually.

Revelation 4:11 (NIV) states, "You are worthy, our Lord and God, to receive glory and honor and power, for you created all things, and by your will they were created and have their being." (See also, Psalm 23; Revelation 3:20–21.)

<u>Prayer</u>
Good morning, my Lord and Master. Truly, I am thankful that you have given me the assurance that because You are guiding me, I need not fear or become overly concerned. You are in every detail of my life and so I have made the choice for You to reign strong in all situations. Bless the Lord! Amen.

WEEK 22

GOD IS A GOD OF NEW BEGINNINGS

Remind yourself of

Experiences with God, the

Mighty God who gave Jesus for

Eternal life to those who believe.

Moments when He brought you out

Before disasters or death struck.

Ever-present One who protects.

Receive His invitation for a new journey.

1 Thessalonians 1:2–5 (NIV) states, "We always thank God for all of you, mention you in our prayers. We continually remember before our God and Father your work produced by faith, your labor prompted by love, and your endurance inspired by hope in our Lord Jesus Christ. For we know, brothers loved by God, that he has chosen you, because our gospel came to you not simply with words, but also with power, with the Holy Spirit and with deep conviction. You know how we lived among you for your sake."

(See also, Isaiah 43.)

Prayer
My Great God, I am very happy that Jesus is the vine and we are the branches and because of that, my substance and sustenance come from Him. I know that to be separated from Jesus is death. Daily, I choose to live for You, as I stay on the vine, Jesus. Praise Him for his excellent greatness! Amen!

GIVE GOD A CHANCE IN YOUR LIFE

Why should you interfere with your life?
Why should you dictate to your Maker the way
You would like your life to be guided?
Don't you know that you are not belonging to yourself?

God has given you the breath that you have.
You have no idea when it will leave you.
There is a divine blueprint for each of God's people.

Did you say, "Father I'll go where you want me to go and
I'll do what you want me to do," before you went ahead and
followed the plans that your mind demands?
You always sought to follow Christ, why go off on a tangent?

Don't worry and ask yourself, "How can I know God's will for my life?"
Just rest back and relax in His arms and say, "God here is my life, let it be consecrated to you." Delight yourself also in the Lord, and He shall give you the desires of your heart.

Because you've been relaxed in His arms and available to him, your heart's desires are guided by Him.
The Lord knows our sorrows. He records our tears,
He takes note of our down sittings and our uprisings.

All our thoughts, our ways and our words are known to Him.
A book of remembrance is written before Him for those who
Fear the Lord and think upon His name.
Perhaps several paths lie ahead, each one open and inviting,
but we need not fear that we shall make a mistake.

It is written, "He shall direct thy paths."
Although you might go through heart breaking situations,
Stay in the will of God.
He may lead you around a path but He is always right.

And remember, everything that happens to you,
Works together for good because
You love and serve the Lord.

Psalm 37:3–11(NIV) states, "Trust in the LORD and do good; dwell in the land and enjoy safe pasture. Delight yourself in the LORD and he will give you the desires of your heart. Commit your way to the LORD; trust in him and he will do this: He will make your righteousness shine like the dawn, the justice of your cause like the noonday sun. Be still before the LORD and wait patiently for him; do not fret when men succeed in their ways, when they carry out their wicked schemes. Refrain from anger and turn from wrath; do not fret—it leads only to evil. For evil men will be cut off, but those who hope in the LORD will inherit the land. A little while, and the wicked will be no more; though you look for them, they will not be found. But the meek will inherit the land and enjoy great peace. The wicked plot against the righteous."

(See also, Hebrews 4:9.)

<u>Prayer</u>

Heavenly Father, I appreciate you for your goodness and love. Faithful are You, O God. I am happy that You never go back on Your promise. Thank you for guiding my footsteps and giving me the assurance that my times are in Your hands. In Jesus name. Amen.

FRAGRANCE

Faithfulness in

Rendering

All areas of my life and

Gracefully, without

Reservation, as an aroma

Ascending to the

Nostrils of my

Creator who provides the

Essence, as the Great Apothecary.

Ephesians 5:2 (NIV) states, "And live a life of love, just as Christ loved us and gave Himself up for us as a fragrant offering and sacrifice to God."

(See also, Matthew 25:23; Luke 16:10–13.)

Prayer
I love you Lord, and I lift my voice to You. I praise Your name because it is great to be praised. My desire is to let my lifestyle be a sweet-smelling fragrance to You. Teach me Your ways so that as I live, others will see You in me and be led to You, for Your honor and glory. Amen!

WEEK 23

PASSION

Pursuing God's purpose for your life with the

Assurance that you are chosen by God and specifically

Selected by Him to

Spread the good news of salvation and to win the lost at any cost.

Impacting the world with a live sermon is matching your walk with your talk.

Overcoming the test of compromising circumstances builds a reputation of integrity.

Never looking back but looking ahead and staying focused on the Great Day of the Lord, Our Messiah when He returns for the saints who have been passionate for His cause.

Jeremiah 29:11–14a (NIV), "'For I know the plans I have for you,'" declares the LORD, "plans to prosper you and not to harm you, plans to give you hope and a future. Then you will call upon me and come and pray to me, and I will listen to you. You will seek me and find me when you seek me with all your heart. I will be found by you," declares the Lord, "and will bring you back from captivity."'

(See also, John 15:16, 19; Peter 2:4; Romans 12:21; Revelation 12:11.)

<u>Prayer</u>

In Jesus' name, I come to You my great Lord and Master, knowing that You are the Author and the Finisher of my faith. Thank you very much for helping me to grow in grace and to let Your light shine in me as I daily seek the knowledge of Your word, that I may be a living sermon for Your honor and glory. Amen.

FISHERS OF MEN

Fishers of men, Jesus called us to go

Into the

Sea of people of various cultures to prepare them for

Heaven.

Matthew 4:19–20 (NIV) states, "'Come, follow me,'" Jesus said, 'and I will make you fishers of men.' At once they left their nets and followed him."

(See also, Mark 1:17; John 21:13–19.)

Prayer

Lord, You are great! You are awesome in this place! I thank you for Your omniscience and Your omnipotence—You know everything and You are everywhere at the same time. Father God, in the name of Jesus, let me not take any moment in time for granted. Give me the boldness to share the gospel message of Jesus to everyone who does not know You, so that they may come to the saving knowledge of Your son, Jesus. Prepare me to be that vessel for Your use. Amen.

INTEGRITY

Intimacy with Christ: Philippians 3:10; Ephesians 3:19; 2 Peter 3:18

Newness in character: Ephesians. 4:24; Romans 6:4; 2 Corinthians 5:17

Truthfulness in lifestyle: Proverbs 8:6; Proverbs 12:19; Zechariah 8:16; Ephesians 4:25

Excellence in the pursuit of life's goals: Isaiah 60:15; Ezekiel 24:21; 2 Corinthians 4:7

Goodness of the heart: Psalm 23:6; Galatians 5:22; Ephesians 5:9

Representative of Christ: 2 Corinthians 5:20; Acts 22:14; Philippians 2:5

Intercession for the soul and spirit of others: Hebrews 7:25; Luke 22:32: Luke 23: 34; John 17:1-11.

Testimony of God-given prosperity: Joshua 1:8-9; Proverbs 19:8; Acts 22:15;

Yielding to Christ: 2 Chronicles 30:8; Romans 6:19; Matthew 12:50; Revelation 22:14

Prayer
I praise and worship you O God, my Father. You are worthy to be praised all day long. I lean on You wholeheartedly to be a person of integrity, because You are the origin of such virtue. I seek Your presence daily so that my life will be a sermon of the integrity of God. I surrender all aspects of my life to You for the excellency of Christ to shine on others for Your honor and glory. Amen.

WEEK 24

DECLARATION OF A WOMAN OF INTEGRITY

Because I am a woman of integrity, I am filled with the fullness of God.
Therefore, I am intimate with Christ, who is my Lover and Lord. To know Him is to love Him unreservedly.

Because I am a woman of integrity, I walk in newness of life and die daily to self by renewing my mind with the Word of God.

Because I am a woman of integrity, I speak the truth, even though it may cause me not to profit monetarily.

Because I am a woman of integrity, I strive for excellence in all my endeavors.
Even if I must try over and again, I will be persistent, because my Father in heaven promises me excellence.

Because I am a woman of integrity, my words and actions characterize goodness, since I will reap whatever I plant. My harvest day is coming.

Because I am a woman of integrity, I am a representative of Christ. I look to Him for love, joy, peace, long-suffering, gentleness, goodness, faith, meekness, temperance and patience.

Because I am a woman of integrity, I intercede for the unsaved, for believers who are weak in the faith, for my enemies, for the Body of Christ, for the unloved and the unlovable.

Because I am a woman of integrity, I live an exemplary lifestyle which is a testimony for others to look at me and say, "I want what she has, I see Jesus in her."

Because I am a woman of integrity, I yield myself to the tender embrace of my Lord and say, "Yes Lord, I will do your will, even if it costs me dearly."

Psalm 25:21 (NIV), "May integrity and uprightness protect me because my hope is in you."

Read also, Romans 13:8-10; Hebrews 13:1-3.

Prayer

You are Lord God, and I bless Your name! I praise You for who You are. You are the glory and the lifter of my head. I worship You because I can totally depend on You. You give me strength, grace and power in the moment when I feel weak. Lord, I thank for sustaining me daily. I lean on You for Godly integrity. Amen.

Alone with God

I like to be alone with God.
It is great to feel His presence
In the cool of the day and
in the stillness of the night.
When the tempter tries to find a loop hole
And wants me to sin,
My blessed Master whispers, "I am with you."

Oh, it's marvelous to inhale the scent
of the Lily of the Valley as He breathes
fresh air upon me and imparts words like,
"Behold I am with you always,
even unto the end of the world."

To be alone with God brings great consolation.
When I am alone with Him I learn to
relax and refrain from worrying.
Lying flat on my belly I converse with Him
while tears trickle down my cheeks.

Father, loving Lord, come close to me.
I want to lose myself and find it in you, to be
victorious over the flesh, the world and Satan.
Then suddenly, that sweet peace that passes
all understanding floods my soul and fills me with more joy.

There is one thing that I admire
about the Creator when I'm with Him.
With His tender and loving hands,
He rolls back the curtains of my memories, shows me

Where He brought me from, where I should be and
What I must be doing.
Then with my heart bowed lowly to my knees,
I say, "Father, please let me not have what I want for my life but

what You know I need for my life."
And O what assurance fills my innermost being
When I hear Him reply, "Well done my child."

Isaiah 51:11 (NIV) states, "Those the LORD has rescued will return. They will enter Zion with singing; everlasting joy will crown their heads. Gladness and joy will overtake them, and sorrow and sighing will flee away".

(See also, Luke 9:18, 36; John 8:29.)

Prayer

Blessed be the name of the Lord. You are great, and worthy to be praised! You are everything to me. There is no word known to man that can adequately describe the communion I experience with You, when I spend time exclusively with You.

Bless the Lord! Please give me what it takes to maintain such quality time with You. Amen.

BREAKTHROUGH

Being in the presence of God and
Remaining ready to
Execute the plans that He births in you,
According to His instructions and to
Keep Him as your source and
Teacher. He gave to you the
Holy Spirit who shall
Reveal the truth about the present for you to
Overcome the strategies of the enemy and to
Understand the revelation of
God as He unveils the wisdom of your
Heavenly calling.

Breakthrough comes from within when you make the choice to listen and obey the voice of God. In so doing, you'll live a lifestyle of walking in the destiny God has ordained for you and the peace of God that passes all human understanding shall be your everlasting portion.

Psalm 140:13 (NIV) states, "Surely the righteous will praise your name and the upright will live before you." (See also Jeremiah 29:11–13; 1 Corinthians 2:9–16.)

<u>Prayer</u>
Thank you, Lord God, that breakthrough comes from You, through Jesus Christ. Teach us to rely on the Holy Spirit to see with spiritual eyes and hear with spiritual ears. Let us be sensitive to Your voice and walk into breakthrough. Amen.

WEEK 25

BRING US DOWN, LORD

Lord, people are way up high
in their haughtiness and pride.
We are superficial in worshipping You.
We sing, but the words are coming
from our lips, not from our hearts.
Your people have gone dry and empty.
Is it really a fashion show on the day of worship?
Or are the cups turned up for Your blessings?

Bring us down O Lord, from our composure,
To help the lost at any cost.
Many are suffering, dying for want of someone
To share love's message.
But Your people are selfish, all for themselves.
Lord, where is the compassion?
Where is the sympathy? All are gone!
Many are striving for power and social status,
And have forgotten the commission
That You gave to them.

Lord bring Your people down,
Let tears flow like a river,
because the eyes are dry.
There are many who are weeping,
whaling and yearning for someone to rescue them.
Oh Jesus, who shall go?
Many are relaxed and quite complacent,
Having everything to their comfort,
While others are experiencing midnight, spiritual midnight.

There are those without clothes and food
Suffering nakedness and malnutrition.
Some are dying and going to eternal damnation.
Bring us down to our knees Lord
Where we can get visions and passion from you.
So that we'll do what you called us to do.

Matthew 28:18-20 (NIV)

Then Jesus came to them and said, "All authority
In heaven and on earth has been given to me
Therefore go and make disciples of all nations,
baptizing them in the name of the father and of
the Son and of the Holy Spirit, and teaching them
to obey everything I have commanded you.
And surely I am with you always, to the very end of the age."

See also, Luke 4:18-19; Luke 9:60; Luke 10:33; Matt. 9:36; 2Timothy 4:2; 1Corinthians 2:1-5

Prayer

Father God, let us never lose sight of the reason you sent Jesus into this world to die a sacrificial death for our sins so that we may be redeemed. He rose from the dead so that we would live eternally with Him. Help us O God, to reach out to others by sharing the Good News of the Gospel to them. Teach us to humble ourselves and put you first in all things for your glory and for our good. In Jesus' name. Amen

ARE YOU READY?

For the defining moment?
For that special interview?
For that final exam?
For that day of delivery?
For the first day of starting your own business?
For the graduation day?
For that day of separation?
For the day when your son or daughter goes off to college?

                         Are **You** Ready?

For your wedding day?
For the doors of your closet of secrets to swing wide open and expose its contents?
For moving in your new home?
For bridging the G-A-P?
For saying goodbye?
For the moment of truth?
For receiving someone who has been long gone out of your life?

                         Are You Ready?

To walk in the destiny that God has for you?
To say, "My stubborn will at last I've yielded"?
To forgive those who wronged you?
To say, "Yes Lord" and mean it?
To do only the will of God for your life?
To take your last breath and to sleep into eternity?
To say, "I have done my best for Jesus."?
To go up with the rapture of the saints?

                         Are You Ready?

"For that great and final day to hear from our Lord God, "Well done" or "I know you not?"

"Are you ready now?"
The level of your readiness determines your fate for eternity.

Matt. 24:37–44 (NIV) states, "As it was in the days of Noah, so it will be at the coming of the Son of Man. For in the days before the flood, people were eating and drinking, marrying and giving in marriage, up to the day Noah entered the ark; and they knew nothing about what would happen until the flood came and took them all away. That is how it will be at the coming of the Son of Man. Two men will be in the field; one will be taken and the other left. Two women will be grinding with a hand mill; one will be taken and the other left."

"Therefore, keep watch, because you do not know on what day your Lord will come. But understand this: If the owner of the house had known at what time of night the thief was coming, he would have kept watch and would not have let his house be broken into. So you also must be ready, because the Son of Man will come at an hour when you do not expect him."

(See also Matthew 25:10; Luke 22:33; Titus 3:1–7.)

Prayer

My everlasting King, You reign over all and You are the keeper of time. Therefore, teach me how to have Godly readiness with my time, talent and other resources that You appointed me to be steward of. Prepare me for every step that I must take to do Your will. In Jesus' name. Amen.x

THE INTANGIBLE

The intangible is invaluable, therefore cannot be bought with silver or gold.

The intangible cannot be explained or fathomed by the mortal human mind.

The intangible is:

- peace of mind
- restful sleep
- giving and receiving forgiveness
- mental coherence
- freedom from emotional abuse
- loving and caring relationships
- freedom in the spirit and soul
- life existing in the blood
- owing no-one anything, but love
- words that bring forth life
- having hope
- giving and receiving grace and mercy
- being delivered from destructive spirits
- the miracle of the cleansing agent of the blood of Jesus and the word of God
- walking and living in newness of life

The intangible originates from the supernatural power of the Almighty God.

John 14:27 (NIV) states," Peace I leave with you; my peace I give you. I do not give to you as the world gives. Do not let your hearts be troubled and do not be afraid."

(See also, John 15:12–15; Ephesians 4:32; 2 Timothy 1:7.)

Prayer

My dear Father God, I love and appreciate You very much for the intangible that comes only from You. It is in Jesus' name that I come boldly in Your presence, knowing that my hope is in You. Thank you for Your strength that prepares me to be a vessel and an instrument for someone else to experience and cherish the intangible. Amen.

WEEK 26

YOU ARE THE GLORY AND THE LIFTER OF MY HEAD

When it seems like midnight all day long,
And it appears that the sun will never shine again,
You are the glory and the lifter of my head.

When I am falsely accused, judged and misjudged,
Because of human manipulation of words,
You are the glory and the lifter of my head.

When lies are being said about me and
Presumptions of my actions become the order of the day,
You are the glory and the lifter of my head.

When my thoughts, mind and heart are misread,
And I am crucified by the human factor,
You are the glory and the lifter of my head.

When my self-esteem is down-trodden and
Beaten because of misunderstandings,
You are the glory and the lifter of my head.

When everything seems to be going right and
It seems like a new dawn is about to break,
But in comes the enemy to crush the dawning of hope,
You are still the
Glory and the lifter of my head.

When humanity is displayed in the form of a mistake
And revenge comes to haunt me day after day,
You are still the glory and the lifter of my head.

When my loved-one looks at me and refers to me
As a "demon" because of a repeated mistake,
You still love me and say I'm valuable.
You are the glory and the lifter of my head.

When memories of actions and words in themselves
Bring back pain in the heart and soul,
You are the glory and the lifter of my head.

When the enemy uses people day after day
To tell me words that paint me as an evil person,
"the victim of generational curses"
I ask myself the question, "Whose report will you believe?"
I boldly say, "I choose to believe that
You are the glory and the lifter of my head."

O Lord my value comes from you.
My security and protection come from you.
My courage comes from you because
You are the glory and the lifter of my head!

Psalm 3:3–8 (NIV) states, "But you are a shield around me, O LORD; you bestow glory on me and lift up my head. To the LORD I cry aloud, and he answers me from his holy hill. I lie down and sleep; I wake again, because the LORD sustains me. I will not fear the tens of thousands drawn up against me on every side. Arise, O LORD! Deliver me, O my God! Strike all my enemies on the jaw; break the teeth of the wicked. From the LORD comes deliverance. May your blessing be on your people."

(See also, Psalm 89:15–17; Philippians 4:19.)

Prayer

Truly Lord, you are my bright morning star, the glory and lifter of my Head. My life is in you. Cause me to make decisions that reflect your glory in my life. I praise and worship you for being with me always. Amen.

DECLARATION OF GOD IN YOUR LIFE

May the almighty

God penetrate the

Light of His countenance in your life so that you will be

Obedient to His call and find

Rest and

Youthfulness, which is unfading life.

Philippians 3:20–21 (NIV) states, "But our citizenship is in heaven. And we eagerly await a Savior from there, the Lord Jesus Christ, who, by the power that enables him to bring everything under his control, will transform our lowly bodies so that they will be like his glorious body."

(See also, Psalm 103:5; Jeremiah 17:7–8.)

Prayer
Jesus, what a wonder you are! You woke me up this morning and clothed me in my right frame of mind. I praise You because You are great. You spoke the world into existence, so I say, be glorified today O God. Amen!

STAND

Suffering long is a gift given by the Holy Spirit so that we can experience the fellowship of Christ's suffering, which brings us into intimacy with Him.

Temperance is a fruit that gives us the ability to control ourselves so that we will look before we leap.

Authority is given to us to cast out demons and everything that exalts itself against who Jesus says we are.

Never give up when the battle is raging because victory is closer than we think.

Dare to look the enemy in his face and see him as he really is, "a defeated foe," He has already been eternally damned by our supreme Judge and General, Christ Jesus.

Galatians 5:22–23 (NIV), "But the fruit of the Spirit is love, joy, peace patience, kindness, goodness, faithfulness, gentleness and self-control. Against such things there is no law."

(See also, Philippians 3:10; Philippians 4:1, 8; Romans 8:35–39.)

Prayer

Lord, I praise You with my whole being. I thank you that You made us victorious over works of the flesh and the enemy of our souls. You can prevent us from falling and so, in your name, I stand against the strategies of the enemy and tear down everything that exalts itself above the name of Jesus. I thank you Lord God, that every knee shall bow, and every tongue shall confess that you are Lord. In Jesus' name. Amen.

WEEK 27

THANKS

To express gratitude from the

Heart for

All things

Notwithstanding the

Kind of circumstances, just

Say thanks!

Philippians 4:6 (NIV) states, "Do not be anxious about anything, but in everything, by prayer and petition, with thanksgiving, present your requests to God."

(Also see, Ephesians 5:20; Psalm 107:21–22.)

Prayer

Lord, you are great, and I bless your name! This is the day that You have made, and I shall rejoice in it. I thank you for all things great and small. New every morning is Your love. Your grace is sufficient to keep us. Amen.

SURRENDER

Stewardship of time, talent and money results in prosperity.

Unite with the Trinity and the body of Christ (spend time in His presence) and the

Righteousness of God will guide you in all things (integrity).

Restore the rejected (discouraged Christians).

Evangelize the lost.

Nourish those who are weak in spirit and (feed the spiritually hungry).

Die daily to self and be devoted unreservedly to God.

Evaluate yourself, "Am I God-focused or people focused?"

Rescue the perishing and give them the light of life.

Psalm 25:21 (NIV) states, "May integrity and uprightness protect me, because my hope, LORD, is in you."

(See also, Galatians 6:1; 1 Corinthians 15:31; 1 Timothy 6:20; 1 Peter 4:10.)

<u>Prayer</u>
Dear Lord, my Father I love and appreciate You. I surrender my will and my emotions. Everything that I possess belongs to You. So, I will rejoice in You because I appreciate every gift that You have given. Amen.

WEEK 28

THE BLOOD OF JESUS

That rich thick blood which was shed on
Calvary's cruel cross is rich with redemption,
Sanctification and transformation.

That royal blood which saves from the gutter-most to the uttermost
Promotes one from the almshouse to the King's house,
From the ditch of sin to the pulpit of righteousness.

Oh, that powerful and precious blood provides healing material
To bind the bruised and broken, to soothe the wounds and aches
That were inflicted by the devil's instruments.

The rich blood of Jesus with its paradoxical function
Washes the heart and changes it from its darkened colors of sin
To white as wool, which signifies purity.

The blood of Jesus is efficacious and far-reaching,
So, reach out and experience a new life after being washed
By that miraculous blood.

John 19:34 (NIV) states, "Instead, one of the soldiers pierced Jesus' side with a spear, bringing a sudden flow of blood and water."

(See also, 1 Peter 1:19; Revelation 12:11.)

Prayer

Father God, I thank you very much for Your goodness, love and mercy. I appreciate You for giving us your Son, Jesus, who sacrificially died for us so that we can have forgiveness of sins. There is such freedom and peace in Jesus and so I depend on Him for healing in the body and mind. His blood was shed for my forgiveness and healing so I walk in victory today. Amen.

EASTER IS FOR OUR REDEMPTION

Ever-loving God sent Jesus to

Atone for the sins of the world so that we may have

Salvation and eternal life and to have the

Terrestrial body in which there is no sorrow or pain.

Everlasting joy and peace shall be for those who are redeemed and

Resurrected with Jesus for a new life in Him.

John 3:16 (NIV) states, "For God so loved the world that he gave his one and only Son, that whoever believes in him shall not perish but have eternal life." (See also, 1 Corinthians 15:40.)

<u>Prayer</u>

O how I love You, Jesus! There is none like You. You are more precious than silver or gold, platinum or diamond. So, I bless Your great name! You took my place; You bought my blame. You made me a new creature. Lord I praise you! Amen.

WEEK 29

GOD IS MY VINDICATOR

Victorious Lord and King, the Judge of my life who clears me of accusations and blame with supporting evidence.

Invincible and Invisible One, who is unconquerable as He fights my battles and makes me an overcomer.

Never-ending Master is He to me.

Day to day the same.

Insurance for life and health.

Comforting One and third in the God head

Activator of energy and strength.

Truth, way and life, therefore He knows what's true.

Overcomer of evil and iniquity.

Redeeming Word to the mind, soul and spirit.

Isaiah 41:10 (NIV) states, "So do not fear, for I am with you; do not be dismayed for I am your God. I will strengthen you and help you; I will uphold you with my righteous right hand."

(See also, Exodus 33:22; Psalm 37:28.)

Prayer

Lord God, what a wonder You are. You are truly amazing! You are the bridge over troubled water. You bring peace in the storm. You are my great defense. I love You. I thank you very much for who You are. Hallelujah! Amen.

BEING SECURE IN CHRIST GUARANTEES SUCCESS

Stability in character

Efficient with resources

Consistency in lifestyle

Unity evidenced in team work

Rest in the spirit, mind and emotions

Excellence in performance.

1 Corinthians 15:57–58 (NIV) "But thanks be to God! He gives us the victory through our Lord Jesus Christ. Therefore, my dear brothers, stand firm. Let nothing move you. Always give yourselves fully to the work of the Lord, because you know that your labor in the Lord is not in vain."

Ephesians 4:7, 11–16 (NIV) "But to each one of us grace has been given as Christ apportioned it. It wasn't me who gave some to be apostles, some to be prophets, some to be evangelists, and some to be pastors and teachers, to prepare God's people for works of service, so that the body of Christ may be built up until we all reach unity in the faith and in the knowledge of the Son of God and become mature, attaining to the whole measure of the fullness of Christ. Then we will no longer be infants, tossed back and forth by the waves, and blown here and there by every wind of teaching and by the cunning and craftiness of men in their deceitful scheming. Instead, speaking the truth in love, we will in all things grow up into him who is the Head, that is, Christ. From him the whole body, joined and held together by every supporting ligament, grows and builds itself up in love, as each part does its work."

(See also, Hebrews 10:23; 1 Thessalonians 2:13; John 17:9–16; Psalm 37:7; Hebrews 4:9; Psalm 8:1, 9; Daniel 5:12; Romans 8:33–37.)

Prayer

I praise and adore you my Lord. You are everything to me and so I bless Your great and mighty name. Thank you for the deep settled peace that comes with knowing You. When we are secure in You, no darts from the enemy will penetrate our shield. Amen.

WEEK 30

WORDS

Wisdom with words

Overcomes,

Redeems, restores, rejuvenates, and makes us

Dead to sin because those words are

Seasoned with salt.

James 1:5 (NIV) states, "If any of you lacks wisdom, he should ask God, who gives generously to all without finding fault, and it will be given to him."

Proverbs 3:13–18 (NIV) states, "Blessed is the man who finds wisdom, the man who gains understanding, for she is more profitable than silver and yields better returns than gold. She is more precious than rubies; nothing you desire can compare with her. Long life is in her right hand; in her left hand are riches and honor. Her ways are pleasant ways, and all her paths are peace. She is a tree of life to those who embrace her; those who lay hold of her will be blessed."

(See also, Proverbs. 4:5–9; Revelations 12:11; Romans 6:11; Colossians 4:6.)

Prayer
Father God, I thank you for Your word which is spirit and life. Teach me to choose my words carefully so that they will reflect the character of Jesus, my Lord. Let my words bring life to those who hears them. In Jesus' name Amen.

TONGUE

Truth or lie, life or death

Outpours from the abundance of the heart.

Never moves until the owner makes the decision to do so.

Give good news or bad news, positive words or negative words.

Under-girding with intercession for the lovely and the unlovely alike, the owner must choose the

Everlasting will of God which is to speak good health and well-being in order to build up and not to tear down.

Philippians 2:10-11 (NIV) "...that at the name of Jesus every knee should bow, in heaven and on earth and under the earth, and every tongue confess that Jesus Christ is Lord, to the glory of God the Father.

(See also, Proverbs 12:18; Proverbs 21:23; James 3:5–5

Prayer

Heavenly Father, the Maker of my life, I thank you that You've given me the ability to choose. But I need You to help me choose godly things. Teach me to constantly use my tongue for the will of God, to build up and not tear down, even if others use theirs to tear me down. In the name of Jesus, I confound every lying tongue and every vessel used by satan to destroy my self-esteem, because greater is He that is within me, than he that is in the world. Amen.

WEEK 31

THE TONGUE IS CONTROLLED BY THE SPEAKER

The tongue can be deadly when used hastily with the shotgun of anger
coming from the emotions.
So, count to ten backwards slowly, before reacting to someone who spoke
harsh and piercing words to
you because during that span of time disaster could be prevented.

Words are carried by the tongue from the thoughts that are generated within.
So, instead of imputing and developing negative thoughts, seek to renew
your mind daily with positive and wholesome thoughts formed from God's
word to build and not to destroy.

Our words reflect our character. They paint a picture of who we truly are,
especially when we are caught off guard.
Let us not spend our lifetime convincing ourselves that words are not seeds
that can take root and grow in our souls and spirits to produce success or failure, life and death.

We must weigh our words carefully and choose to ask ourselves before we speak,
"Will I cause someone to waiver in his faith in God?"
"Will I try to have my way through manipulation?"

"Will my words inspire, motivate, encourage or discourage the listener?"

The tongue is controlled by the speaker, therefore, let us choose to speak words
  that reflect the character of Christ since we are His disciples who have
  been regenerated by the redemptive power of His blood that was shed.

We must daily, choose to speak words of life and healing,
words of praise and honor to God, words of grace and blessing,
words of wisdom and edification, words of peace and loving correction,
  words that motivate and stir up confidence and the gifts
  God gave us.

Psalm 119:13 states, "With my lips, I recount all the laws that come from your mouth."

Colossians 3:16 states, "Let the word of Christ dwell in you richly as you teach and admonish one another with all wisdom, and as you sing Psalms and spiritual songs with gratitude in your hearts to God."

(See also Colossians 4:6.)

Prayer
Yahweh, you are the absolute faithful God in whom I place my trust. Please help me to live my life with words, seasoned with your never-failing grace. Amen!

Anointing

Allowing the Holy Spirit to empty us of our selfish desires and motives, for us to experience a fresh and

New outpouring of His presence as He fills us supernaturally with the

Oil of gladness and the powerful fragrance that comes from being in an

Intimate relationship with Him.

Never sacrificing precious moments with God for traditions of men and mundane rituals of religiosity.

Taking time out daily to develop a lifestyle of worship, which will take us in the

Inner-court where we'll experience a taste of His glory which will prepare us for seemingly,

Never-ending battles during our earthly journey, over which

God made us more than conquerors.

1 John 2:27 (NIV) states, "As for you, the anointing you received from him remains in you, and you do not need anyone to teach you. But as his anointing teaches you about all things and as that anointing is real, not counterfeit—just as it has taught you, remain in him."

(See also, Psalm 45:7; Psalm 92:10; 2 Corinthians 1:21.)

Prayer

Thank you, Lord for Your awesome presence. Your glory is what I yearn for in my life. Because when Your glory penetrates this flesh, my spirit is renewed and a new desire for more of You is continuously on the increase. I praise You, Father, for making Yourself real to me. Amen.

WEEK 32

WAKE UP

Watch God

Activate His

Kingdom principles in your life as you invest

Early morning time with Him.

Utilize every minute of that moment to tap into God's

Precious presence where you'll find fullness of joy and strength, to face and overcome the challenges of your day.

Psalm 89:15 (NIV) states, "Blessed are those who have learned to acclaim you, who walk in the light of your presence, O LORD."

(See also, Psalm 63:1; Luke 10:9, 12:13; Luke 17:21; 2 Timothy 2:15.)

Prayer

Bless the Lord, o my soul and all that is within me! Truly Lord, Your promises are stronger and more stable than a rock. You honor Your word above Your name and so I stand on Your word that never lies because it's spirit and life. Amen.

Successful Transition Takes Time

Transition starts with taking an
Introspective look at ourselves and
Seeing who we really are.
Looking at the deep recesses of our heart
And setting the mirror in the position
Where all details, positive and negative,
Are revealed to only us.
Then we arrive at a moment in time,
When we must make a crucial decision to
Change the character that we see and
Start the process of being conformed to
The image of Jesus, our Lord and Master.

Transition begins when we make a choice to
Spend time with God as the first activity of our day.
Making the decision to be obedient to His word as
We read and meditate on it daily.
Choosing to live a life of gratitude so that
Our attitude will radiate as a beam of
Light piercing through to the hearts that
Have not been saturated with thankfulness.
That change will start us on a new journey to discover our real purpose.

Acknowledging that God is our source and we
Depend totally on Him, we choose to
Live a life of worship, in recognition of who He is.
Transition occurs when, because of our intimate
Relationship with Christ, we choose to rise above
The trivialities of the world's system and see
People how Jesus sees them.
Our mission will become people-focused rather than
self-focused for the glory of God.

When we make the transition, we will live a
Victorious lifestyle because we choose to walk
In the kingdom of God, where it's not meat or drink,
But righteousness, peace and joy in the Holy Ghost.
It takes time to transition.
Will you take time to invest in the process
Of change in order to experience the true
Intimacy that comes from knowing Jesus, our
Redeemer and Lord?

2 Chronicles 7:14 (NIV) states, "If my people, who are called by my name, will humble themselves and pray and seek my face and turn from their wicked ways, then will I hear from heaven and will forgive their sin and will heal their land."

Psalm 119:10 (NIV) states, "I seek you with all my heart; do not let me stray from your commands."

(See also, Matthew 6:33; Romans 14:17; Jeremiah 7:23; Deuteronomy 13:4.)

Prayer

I thank you Lord that there is freedom in knowing You. We look above the trite and mundane things of this world's system and focus on the most important things of life. I appreciate You for making us realize through Your word that we must seek You and Your kingdom first, above all things. In You are all things, so we walk in Your fullness as we seek You daily. Bless the Lord! Amen.

WEEK 33

HOLY SPIRIT YOU ARE WELCOME IN MY LIFE

Welcome Holy Spirit!
Come and fill me with your awesome presence
that gives me never-ending assurance and comfort.
Brighten my days and bring me to a dimension
that no man or woman can elevate me to.
You are welcome in my life.

O what great consolation it is to know
that You are always here to brush my fears away.
You also dry the tears that roll down to my cheeks.
My strength is in You, my hope is in You.
Precious guide and revealer of my life, I adore You!
You are most welcome in my life.

Holy Spirit please show me exactly
what I must do in order to please You.
Help me not to quench You because
You are the flowing stream that comes from within me,
And continues to revive and rejuvenate my spiritual cells.
Without You, I can do nothing O my Great Teacher.
You are welcome in my life.

You are the fire that burns
every dross of sin known and unknown to me.
You are the dove that glides and flutters
in my innermost being and controls my emotions.
You are the fountain that continues to well up within me,
and refreshes me daily.
You are most welcome in my life!

Ephesians 1:13 (NIV) states, "And you also were included in Christ when you heard the word of truth, the gospel of your salvation. Having believed, you were marked in Him with a seal, the promised Holy Spirit."

(See also, Romans 14:17; Psalm 51:11.)

Prayer

Surely, You are my everlasting King and my portion! Hallelujah to Your great and powerful name, Jesus! You are more precious that silver, gold or platinum. I bless Your mighty Name! Amen.

WOMAN

Wisdom— Understanding of what is true, right; good judgement. Characterized by virtues such as honesty, sobriety, chastity, concern for good reputation.
Proverbs 4:5–9
Proverbs 14:1, 12:4

Olive Oil— Soothing and curative; main ingredient of soap. Gives flavor; source of light. Leviticus 24:2
Psalm 23:5
James 5:14

Mercy— Compassion; A disposition to be kind and forgiving.
Proverbs 3:3, 11:17

Anointing— To apply oil; set apart for sacred use.
Power of God; Burden removing; Yoke destroying.
2 Corinthians 1:12
Isaiah 10:27

Nobility— Illustrious
Greatness of character; Stately and magnificent
Acts 17:11
Proverbs 3:3, 11:17

Prayer

My Lord and Master, You are the Great Physician who performed the first surgery—by putting man to sleep and removing a rib from his side in order to create woman. A woman is extremely special to You. So, there are details about a woman that are exclusive to You. You made her as the man's Ebenezer, or helper. When You skillfully created woman, You placed in her invaluable gifts not known to man. That is the reason I am so deeply attracted to You and in love with You. Bless the Lord, O my soul! I praise you my Father! Amen.

DECLARATION OF WHO I AM

A female, created in God's image, God skillfully handcrafted me.

A Godly woman who is called to be like Christ, rich with beauty that never goes unnoticed.

A daughter, the blessed fruit of my mother's womb.

A mother, whom my children look at and call "blessed."

A worker and business woman, called to occupy till Jesus comes, and to make a positive difference in my world.

A sister, united in the bond of love and peace.

A godly wife, who wins my husband with my good conduct and fervent prayers.

I am an effective manager of my time and my finances.

I am a sower of good and positive seeds, because whatever I sow, that will I reap.

I am a woman of wisdom, in my left hand there is riches and honor in my right hand there is length of days.

I am a soul winner; therefore, I am wise.

I am a word-warrior; therefore, I hide God's word in my heart that I'll not sin against Him.

I am a woman of excellence; therefore, I do not settle for mediocrity because I serve a God of excellence.

2 Timothy 2:15 (NIV) states, "Do your best to present yourself to God as one approved, a workman who does not need to be ashamed and who correctly handles the word of truth." (See also, Galatians 6:7–10; Proverbs 31:1-31

Prayer

Dearest Father and Lord of my life, I appreciate You for being who You are. Since You came into my life, You've made everything new and placed a new perspective in my mind-set for me to see the value You've created within me, from the foundation of the Earth. El Shaddai, please cause me to make a positive difference everywhere I go for Your honor and glory. Amen.

WEEK 34

DISCIPLINE

Decisions that will dictate our destiny made on the battlefield of the mind are

Instilled and imprinted on our souls to

Surrender and bring under subjection to the Holy Spirit, our mind, will, and emotions so that self-

Control will be the order of the day as the

Inner-man is set apart for the glory of God. We must bring

Pleasure to the

Lord and Master of our lives as He develops the

Intellect and builds our character, when we submit to the Holy Spirit who brings

Nobility and

Excellence in our lives.

John 8:31 (NIV) states, "To the Jews who had believed him, Jesus said, "If you hold to my teaching, you are really my disciples."

(See also, Psalm 147:11; Psalm149:4; Ephesians 1:5; Revelation 4:11.)

Prayer

Blessed be the name of the Lord. You are worthy to receive honor and glory, majesty, dominion and power. In the name of Jesus, I thank you my Father for giving me the opportunity for sharing Your love with others. As I live for You daily, cause me to live a life of discipline, so others will see a sermon and be led to follow You, for Your honor and glory. Amen.

TEARS

Shall we shed tears of sorrow, regret or joy?

Yes, it's human to shed tears, but do we

Experience pain, anger or gladness in the process?

Sometimes tears speak louder than words.

Let's turn the circumstances of those tears that are not "joy tears"

Into the opportunities to hear what God is saying in the circumstances.

Tears, a language God understands, as they eke from the

Emotions, are a God-given characteristic of humanity which reflect the

Attitudes toward life's circumstances. Although only God knows the heart, those attitudes are often misunderstood by the on-looker, but we need not fear because our Vindicator is with us.

Reach into the spirit-man, where God has embedded in us all His attributes and conquer the challenges and crises that pull at our heart strings.

Supernaturally, God will undergird us and cause us to find peace and joy sublime, so that we will gain strength to rise above the lies of our enemy, the devil, to be winners and victorious over the next challenge that life may present to us.

Psalm 126:5 (NIV) states, "Those who sow in tears shall reap with songs of joy." (See also, Psalm 56:8.)

Prayer

Precious Lord and Master, I am thankful that You are the source of joy. I appreciate You for understanding me the way you do. You are always there when things go wrong, and You dry the tears from my eyes. You are worthy to be praised. Amen.

WEEK 35

THOUGHTS

Think with all the emotions, running, skipping, blazing and going wild all at once in a

House not made with human hands.

Overcome by imaginations that may be real, true or just complete lies and sometimes mixed with misunderstandings of the images portrayed.

Underestimating the love and power of God who made us more than conquerors in Him.

Give it up! Pull them down! All struggles that seem like a jigsaw puzzle or perhaps like cobwebs.

Heaven, with all its angelic beings and Jesus, the center of their attention bids you to

Treasure in your mind and spirit the love relationship that prompts you to adore and express to the lover of your soul, how much you appreciate Him because He is your

Source and complete satisfaction.

2 Corinthians 10:3–5: "For though we live in the world, we do not wage war as the world does. The weapons we fight with are not the weapons of the world. On the contrary, they have divine power to demolish strongholds. We demolish arguments and every pretension that sets itself up against the knowledge of God, and we take captive every thought to make it obedient to Christ."

Prayer

Lord I thank you that You are concerned about every detail of our lives. So, I commit all my thoughts and emotions, both negative and positive, to You. Cause me to think on the things that are lovely and of good report to the honor and glory of Your name. Amen.

OFFENSE

The act of striking against. The act of attacking or assaulting.

Overacting to statements and actions from others

Far beyond the intent of the alleged offenders

Face the inner-man boldly and

Eradicate, with the help of the Holy Spirit, the

Noisome insecurities that plague you and

Stand firm with soundness of character and not be swayed by

Every suspicious appearance and sound of speech.

The Holy Spirit is your Revealer and God is your Vindicator.

Matthew 11:6 states, "And blessed is he who shall not be offended in me."

<u>Prayer</u>

Father God I bless Your Holy name! You are good and your mercies endure forever. I thank you because You are our protection, our vindicator, and our strong tower. We run to Your place of refuge, and we are saved. Bless the Lord. Amen.

WEEK 36

SERVE GOD

Satisfy your Maker with the substance

Endowed upon you for the purpose of reaching people with His love.

Realize that in utilizing your gifts you open the doors to

Victory, which is the key to

Enriching and elevating the recipients of the fruits of your lips and hands for the

Glory of God, your Father, who will

Overtake you with spiritual blessings because you are

Devoted to His purpose and fulfilling His will.

1 Samuel 12:24 (NIV) "But be sure to fear the Lord and serve Him faithfully with all your heart; consider what great things He has done for you."

(See also Matthew 4:10; Hebrews 9:14)

Prayer
Bless the Lord, O my soul, and all that is within me. Dear Lord, it is so great to know You, because to know You, is to serve You. I take pleasure in representing You today and always. Thank you for giving me opportunities for serving others because that's how I serve You. Amen.

How to Invoke Respect

Rule out all differences and remember that every individual is God's creation.

Establish a system of honor in order to

Support, strengthen and value the

Person's position, gifts and needs.

Extinguish selfish ambitions and desires.

Capture and cultivate the attitude of gratitude, then you will

Transition from indifference to glorifying God with the fruits of your lips and actions.

1 Peter 2:17 (NIV) states, "Show proper respect to everyone: Love the brotherhood of believers, fear God and honor the king."

(See also, Psalm 74:20, 119:4–7; Romans 13:7; Philippians 4:13; 1Timothy 5:17).

Prayer

Blessed be the name of the Lord. Father God, worthy are You to receive honor, glory, dominion and power, because you are most High! Thank you very much for revealing Yourself through Your holy word. Teach us to be keenly aware of those written principles and the wisdom to implement them in our day to day lives, so we will bring honor to Your name as we invoke respect. It is in the name of Jesus that I present my heart's desire. Amen.

WEEK 37

ACCOUNTABILITY

Accounting for our actions and resources by being

Conscious of the fact that God is omnipresent and omniscient. Therefore, we must be

Committed to control our emotions and

Occupy the position of being good stewards of the resources that God gave us.

Understanding that we must appear before the judgement seat of Christ to receive justice for all we've done.

Not pointing fingers at others for the wrong they've done without the opportunity for reconciliation.

Thoughts brought under subjection to think of only those things that are of good report.

Always staying focused on the purpose of our being.

Build our character with the word of God daily, as we become more

Intimate with Jesus our

Lord and master who will

Inspire us to

Teach others about

Yielding their lives unreservedly to the will of God.

Matthew 12:35–37 (NIV) states, "The good man brings good things out of the good stored up in him, and the evil man brings evil things out of the evil stored up in him. But I tell you that men will have to give account on the Day of Judgment for every careless word they have spoken. For by your words you will be acquitted and by your words you will be condemned."

Philippians 4:9 (NIV) states, "Whatever you have learned or received or heard from me, or seen in me—put it into practice. And the God of peace will be with you."

(See also, 1 Corinthians 4:5; 2 Corinthians 5:10.)

Prayer

Thank you, Lord that there is a way out of our will and self-focus. Jesus is the way that You provided for us. He came to save us from the self-destruction. Let Your Holy Spirit draw us to You so that we still walk in Your will and Your way. Amen.

Are You a Giver or a Taker?

A giver is a person who:

- Gives cheerfully and without regret.
- Takes pleasure in giving and will not announce the act of giving to everyone else so that, they will know that they are always giving.
- Gives without stipulating the conditions by which the gift will be given
- Gives regardless of peoples' opinions.
- Is thankful for God's provisions and learns to be content with what he or she possesses.
- Has the heart and attitude to share and will, without hesitation, share what is given to him or her so that another person's need can be met.
- Takes nothing for granted and lives a lifestyle of gratitude.

A taker is a person who:

- Always expects something from people.
- Takes everything for granted, and forgets very quickly about every gift that God has given to him or her.
- Scrutinizes and criticizes gifts received and tries to assess their value in a critical manner.
- Is jealous and envious of others' possessions
- Thinks that others are indebted to him or her and always because of a favor he or she granted many years ago.
- Gives so that others may see and publicly commend him or her.
- Becomes confrontational when asked to repay a debt owed.
- Takes credit for the work that someone else did, in order to receive praise and commendation.

The giver shall flourish like a tree planted by the rivers of water that bring forth fruit in its season. The taker shall gather crops and put its proceeds in his pockets with holes.

Luke 6:38 (NIV) states, "Give, and it will be given to you. A good measure, pressed down, shaken together and running over, will be poured into your lap. For with the measure you use, it will be measured to you." (See also, Acts 20:35; Malachi 3:8–12.)

Prayer

Heavenly Father, I appreciate You very much because You are the Supreme Giver. You truly thought of us for sacrificial giving. So, let us understand the true meaning of giving so that we will experience Your glory and the true presence of God because it is more blessed to give than to receive. I thank you, Lord, that all resources come from You and the more we give, You will multiply them. Hallelujah to the lamb of God! Amen.

WEEK 38

HIS MAJESTY

He reigns supreme over all the earth and with supernatural

Intelligence that no human mind can fathom

Superstar among all stars in the heavenly realm where there is no competition with illumination

Mover of all mountains in the lives of people residing in the earthly realm.

Awesome and glorious in countenance that would consume us and so, like Moses, God covers us with His hand as He passes by.

Justifier of those who receive salvation through His Son, Jesus.

Ever reigning in His kingdom that shall never end. He is enthroned with His

Scepter of righteousness. He is majestic

Throughout all the ages and all who serve Him, honor and worship His name shall see Him in all His splendor because He truly reigns

Yesterday, today and forever. He is our King eternal.

Hebrews 1:7–9 (NIV) states, "In speaking of the angels he says, 'He makes his angels winds, his servants flames of fire.' But about the Son he says, 'Your throne, O God, will last forever and ever, and righteousness will be the scepter of your kingdom. You have loved righteousness and hated wickedness; therefore God, your God, has set you above your companions by anointing you with the oil of joy.'"

(See also, Psalm 95:1-6; Psalm 9:1-13; 2Thessalonians 1:8-12.)

<u>Prayer</u>
Lord, You are worthy to be praised and adored. You are an awesome God! You are high, above all gods. Blessed be Your holy name! Heaven and Earth are in awe of Your glory, which covers the heavens and the Earth. Hallelujah!
Amen!

THE SANCTUARY OF GOD

This is the place where the presence of
God lives in my spirit.
I make myself go to that place in the
midst of the hustle and bustle,
struggles and challenges of life, where I find rest and peace that
only Jesus gives.

This is the place where I find refuge for my soul
and the healing balm, where the waters flow
from the river of God that refreshes the
spirit and mind. It provides healing
for sick bodies.

This is the place where the unconditional
love of God originates from, for the discouraged
and the rejected who will hear Jesus say,
"You can only love the unlovely and the
hateful with my love."

This is the place where the heart is purified
because a spiritual blood transfusion takes
place so that deceit, malice and strife will
be eradicated.
Then the heartbeat will echo God's heart
beat, with honesty and unity with the body of Christ.

This is the place where sadness will turn into joy,
and disappointments will appear as opportunities
to wait and to stand still and watch the
faithfulness of God revealed in its time because
God cannot lie.

This is the place where we must surrender
our will and selfish desires, our dislikes
and likes to our Lord Jesus in order to be

stripped of ourselves and be conformed
to the image of Christ.

This is the place where we escape to, so that
we may receive direction and counsel
from our Wonderful Counselor and Mighty God.
This is the place where God the Father, the Son
and the Holy Spirit makes Himself real to me
because I go to that place, the Sanctuary
of God, without reservation.

Psalm 32:7 states, "You are my hiding place, you will protect me from trouble and surround me with songs of deliverance."

(See also, Psalm 31:19–20, 23–24.)

<u>Prayer</u>

Precious Father, you are my God and it is in Jesus' name that I approach your majesty, knowing that You are love, and You care for me enough, to be the glory and the lifter of my head. Thanks for Your protection, provision and providence. Amen!

WEEK 39

ENTER HIS PRESENCE

Position yourself and go into that place where Jesus dwells and you will find

Rest for your weary soul and spirit. His glorious attributes are

Efficacious to soothe your troubled mind because it is in that

Secret place where no one, but the lover of your soul, you will find.

Enter with praise and intimate worship, and the fragrance will capture your beloved.

Nothing else but His holiness and majesty will welcome you to

Celebrate His presence where you'll find strength and

Everlasting joy that flow like a fountain.

Psalm 16:11 (NIV) states, "You have made known to me the path of life; you will fill me with joy in your presence, with eternal pleasures at your right hand."

1 Thessalonians 5:17–18 (NIV) states, "Pray continually; give thanks in all circumstances, for this is God's will for you in Christ Jesus."

Psalm 104:33 (NIV) states, "I will sing to the LORD all my life; I will sing praise to my God as long as I live."

(See also, Psalm 63:3; 1John 3:19-24.)

Prayer

I praise You, Father, for Your loving kindness is better than life. There is protection and assurance when I dwell in Your presence. The peace that surpasses human understanding is unexplainable and so I'll bless Your name forever. Amen!

FAULT-FINDING

Feelings and expressions of dogmatism toward another, enveloped in deep-seated and false sense of

Authority that facades the

Unknown which is the lack of knowledge of all facts.

Letting insecurities overcome the ability to research the

Truth and facts of all variables.

Failing to realize that we all have fallen short since we are finite beings.

Introspectively, we fail to see ourselves as who we really are.

Not stopping to think that there is more to the circumstances.

Doing what God hates and not remembering that we are imperfect people.

Initiating the process of finger-pointing will assist the enemy of our souls to strategize our downfall, at a time when we are vulnerable.

Never stopping to think that it's best for us to not dwell on another's failures, but to pray that they'll come to a place of repentance and be delivered.

Giving the impression to the on-lookers and hearers that all, "is well" when three fingers of the fault-finders are pointing back toward themselves.

Romans 9:18–20 (NIV) states, "Therefore God has mercy on whom he wants to have mercy, and he hardens whom he wants to harden. One of you will say to me: 'Then why does God still blame us? For who resists his will?' 'But who are you, O man, to talk back to God?' Shall what is formed say to him who formed it, 'Why did you make me like this?'"

Job 33:12-13 (NIV) states, "But I tell you, in this you are not right, for God is greater than man. Why do you complain to him that he answers none of man's word?"

James 5:9 (NIV) states, "Don't grumble against each other, brothers, or you will be judged. The Judge is standing at the door!" (See also, 1 Corinthians 10:10.)

<u>Prayer</u>
Father God, I praise You for Your excellent greatness! Teach me Your ways so that I will not sin against You. Cause Your Holy Spirit to let me help to build others' character for reconciliation onto You. Please help us to not be finger-pointers at others, but to be conformed to the image of Christ, so our lives will be sermons that lead them to You.
In Jesus' name. Amen.

WEEK 40

Divert Me, O God

Divert me, O God, from fleshy ungodly thoughts.

Let Your Holy Spirit fire burn within.

Burn every corrupt mental image.

Consume my old sinful nature

that tries to haunt me.

O Holy Ghost, Holy Ghost,

Let the fire fall.

Purify my mind and illuminate my spirit with the light of Your countenance.

O God, my God, divert me for Your honor and glory.

Philippians 4:8 (NIV) states, "Finally, brothers, whatever is true, whatever is noble, whatever is right, whatever is pure, whatever is lovely, whatever is admirable—if anything is excellent or praiseworthy—think about such things. Whatever you have learned or received or heard from me, or seen in me—put it into practice. And the God of peace will be with you."

(See also, Galatians 5:17; Hebrews 12:28-29).

Prayer

I love You, Lord, and I lift my voice to worship You! I adore You and I lay my life before You. O, how I love You. No one else can clean me up like You can. I thank you for the blood of Jesus that washes whiter than snow. Bless the Lord! Amen.

REDEMPTION

I have been bought with the blood of Jesus because I could not pay the debt I incurred.

I am delivered from the enslavement of sin and released to a new freedom.

I have a relationship with God, and a new life in Christ which gives me peace.

I serve my Master and Lord with all God-given gifts.

I give Christ priority in my life. He is the source of my joy and the center of attraction in all I do.

I am safe and secure from all harm because God is my protection.

I shall sit with Abraham, Isaac and Jacob in the Kingdom of Heaven.

I shall wear a white robe, glorify God and sing a new song in the new Jerusalem.

I have experienced the miracle of redemption, have you?

Titus 2:11-14, "For the grace of God that brings salvation has appeared to all men. It teaches us to say "No" to ungodliness and worldly passions, and to live self-controlled, upright and godly lives in this present age, while we wait for the blessed hope---the glorious appearing of our great God and Savior, Jesus Christ, who gave himself for us to redeem us from all wickedness and to purify for himself a people that are his very own, eager to do what is good."

(See also, Isaiah 35:9; 1 Peter 1:18-19; Revelation 5:9, 7–9).

Prayer

Thank you, Lord God, for Your redeeming power through Jesus Christ our Lord. He became sin for me, so I may have the righteousness of God. Please help me, O Father, to live according to Your will and for Your honor and glory. Amen!

WEEK 41

REVIVAL

Resurrected from selfish ambitions and an ungodly lifestyle to

Experience the process of reconciliation to the Holy One, to whom we've made

Vows to follow and do His will, without reservation.

Introspectively, seeing through a spiritual microscope and honestly admitting that we have grieved the Holy Spirit because we have walked away from the holiness of God. We then, with righteous indignation, take a giant step into

Victory and take a stand against the enemy, Satan, because we made a conscious decision to repent of our sinful and evil ways and turn to the God of our salvation where we experience intimate communion with Him.

Availing ourselves to our forgiving God, we become agents of revival with a passion for souls and motivation to lead them to the saving knowledge of Jesus Christ.

Losing our will and dying to ourselves daily, in order to gain the excellency of our redeeming King.

Isaiah 57:15b states, "I live in a high and lowly place, but also with him who is contrite and lowly in spirit, to revive the spirit of the lowly and to revive the heart of the contrite."

(See also, Psalm 19:7.)

Prayer

O river of life, living water, my God and everlasting portion, only You can refresh the spiritually thirsty and revive the spirit of Your people. Thank you for Your refreshing spirit and power that rejuvenate us to do what You want us to do.
In the strong name of Jesus. Amen!

HELPER

Heavenly concept, conceived and created by God of

Equal value with her male partner in the sight of God. Knowing this fully well, she acts wisely as her life shines as the

Light that represents her Maker. It's given to her for the purpose of extinguishing darkness during the midnight of life's circumstances.

Position and profession, so distinctly engineered by her Creator, that there must be no Confusion with the role that she is predestined to perform.

Ebenezer, "a stone of help" that undergirds her mate with intercession and compliments his calling and destiny with her godly virtues, embedded in her character.

Recipient of God's incomparable love, because she is the beloved of the Lord.

Genesis 2:18 states, "The Lord said, it is not good for man to be alone, I will make a helper suitable for him"

(See also, Proverbs 14:1; Proverbs 31:10–12, 23–26.)

Prayer
Thank you, Lord, my God! You are worthy to receive honor, glory and praise. I bless Your holy name today. Hallelujah! You are my rock of stability. I depend on You for my sustenance and inspiration. God You are awesome! Glory to God in the highest! Amen!

WEEK 42

THE JOURNEY IS ROUGH BUT

God is bountiful in grace and mercy to bring us through trying circumstances that seem endless and many times without sunshine.

God is the all-seeing eye that sees and cares about every tear-drop that rolls down your cheeks from being falsely accused.

God is the giver of peace when there are emotional struggles and inner war caused by the voice of another human vessel.

God is the only one who can stop the controlling spirit that seeks to control your thoughts and your desires to aspire toward greatness in Him with your God-given gifts.

God is omniscient, He knows everything about you. In His time, He will ensure that He ends the unrest that continues to plague His beloved.

God is the restorer of the weary and broken. He gives strength and puts back all the pieces as if they were never impaired or injured.

God is the provider of opportunities and He will draw the gifted, but down-trodden to Him, so that the warmth of His love and assurance be intimately known.

God is the shield that prevents the darts of manipulative tactics, jealous innuendos and insecurities of the attacker from piercing through the frame of the spirit-man.

God is your strength when you work tirelessly for an honest living so that others may be happy. When the instruments of the enemy try to carve deep into the core of your being, God will rebuke and destroy that enemy.

God is the purifier of negative deposits and garbage dumped by the enemy through the ear-gates. God's word provides comfort and refurbishes that which was stripped from your spirit.

Truly, the journey is rough but because we are being processed to total trust in God, He will carry us safely to the predestined end for His honor and glory.

Romans 8:38–39 states, "For I am persuaded, that neither death nor life, nor angels, nor principalities, nor powers, nor things present, nor things to come. Nor height nor depth, nor any other creature, shall be able to separate us from the love of God, which is in Christ Jesus, our Lord."

(See also, Psalm 37:3-8.)

<u>Prayer</u>

You are my glorious Father, so I bless Your great and majestic name! I adore You, my Adonai, Lord and Sovereign above all. I appreciate You, for engraving my name in the palm of Your hands. I love You very much for being with me through every step and every transition in my journey of life. In Jesus' name. Amen!

Clean Hands

Consecrated and committed to

Live a lifestyle consistent with the

Eternal principles and precepts of the

Authoritative word of God, which brings about a

Newness in the thought process, in order to prevent deceptive strategies from becoming a reality, which could cause others to become victims.

Hands are made by God as an extension of His hands to carry out His will here on earth,

Assuring that His peoples' needs are met according to the gifts, He gave them.

Nothing is too hard for God to do when we place everything in His hands,

Daily presenting others and ourselves in prayer to Him is a gesture of

Submitting to His will in order to carry out His purpose for His honor and glory.

Psalm 24:4 (NIV) states, "He that hath clean hands, and a pure heart; who hath not lifted up his soul into vanity nor sworn deceitfully. He shall receive the blessing from the Lord, and righteousness from the God of their salvation."

(See also, John 15:3; Psalm 73:1; Isaiah 56:2.)

Prayer

Thank you, Lord, for the opportunities You have provided me to be taught Your uncompromising truth from Scripture. I need Your strength and grace daily to maintain a lifestyle that represents You on this earth. Amen!

WEEK 43

THE LEVIATHAN SPIRIT

Lucifer, the monstrous demonic enemy of the human soul, with his seemingly multiple heads seeks to wreak havoc by assigning his officers to believers who earnestly serve the Lord and desire to do His will.

Ever relentlessly trying to prove his superiority above all others in intellect, knowledge and leadership abilities, if it means demeaning the gifted and the anointed saints with the goal of defeating the divine plan of grace toward mankind and to divert the beloved of God from their destinies.

Vengeance is his delight. Without provocation, he executes it on all his prey who sometimes become victims by his acts of violence and tyranny. He temporarily maintains a calm and unruffled demeanor as a façade among God's people after he orchestrates their demise.

Intimidation is his approach as he initiates dogmatic expressions of presumptions and unwise criticisms of others without reservations. He proceeds as the judge of the heart of others when their actions do not meet his expectations. Like himself, he makes believers transient and confused.

Authority over everyone who is drawn to his seemingly graceful form, is his pursuit. Then behold, his insatiable appetite for control exudes from his pride and arrogance as he constantly and cunningly compares himself with others and seeks for affirmation and glory. Suddenly, the believers find themselves in his jaws.

Thrashing with bellows of threats, sharp, crafty and poisonous words that rip the hearts and souls like a merciless dagger with the intention of terrifying and destroying those who love and serve

God. With such terror he expects his prey to humbly submit to his demands.

Haughtiness is an unclean spirit that God hates, but it characterizes the essence of the leviathan's conversations about material and religious accomplishments and takes full credit for the success of others. "Humility and transparency" become his song so that the naïve will be unquestionably impressed with the smoothness and creativity of his speech.

Alas, he is now calm and composed but no one knows when he'll strike again. We dare not make the mistake of relaxing in our comfort zones because his eyes appear to be closed. But instead, they are roaming all over his territory and beyond. He repeats the vicious cycle of complaining about the inadequacies of others—near and far.

Nevertheless, God is infinitely mighty and more powerful than all His creations. He is the King of glory! He is mighty in battle! God owns the Earth, and the world, and everything in it. He founded it upon the seas and established it upon the waters. We will seek Him with pure hearts in prayer and fasting. We will praise Him all the days of our lives. Though the leviathan spirit advances toward us and tries to attack and devour us, God is our shelter and stronghold because He shall destroy that spirit and we will see it no more.

Ephesians 6:10-13(NIV) states, "Finally, be strong in the Lord and his mighty power. Put on the full armor of God so that you can take your stand against the devil's schemes. For our struggle is not against flesh and blood, but against the rulers, against the authorities, against the powers of this dark world and against the spiritual forces of evil in the heavenly realms. Therefore, put on the full armor of God, so that when the day of evil comes, you may be able to stand your ground, and after you have done everything, to stand."

(See also, Job Chapter 41; Isaiah 27:1; Ephesians 6:12; Psalm 24; Psalm 27:1–2; Psalm 74:14; Proverbs 8:13; Proverbs 16:5,18,19; Proverbs 27:2).

Prayer

Lover of my soul, my heavenly Father, I adore You and appreciate You for loving me with unconditional love. There is no height or depth that supersedes the intensity of Your love for humanity, and for this I am eternally grateful to You. I trust You explicitly for giving me the sensitivity and discernment to recognize the strategy of the enemy, so that I will not become prey, but be victorious because You are victorious. In Jesus' name. Amen!

MIND-READERS

Mind-readers are an abomination to the Lord because they judge others as if they are blameless, even when they are proven wrong by their own findings.

Mind-readers blaspheme the principles of God because they proceed in dealing with others as if they are superior in matters of the spirit.

Mind-readers are critically destructive because they pretend that their history had no darkness and emptiness, as soon as they acquire some degree of material prosperity.

Mind-readers destroy others' self-esteem when they assume or discover that their opinions are not well received because they are harsh and regimental in their approach, especially on issues deemed important to them.

Mind-readers estimate themselves higher than others and take for granted others whom God used to be instrumental in boosting their self-esteem and bringing them into opportunities to utilize their gifts.

Mind-readers are finger-pointers at others' weaknesses and failures yet fail to accept the truth about themselves. With self-righteousness, they condemn those who fail to meet their newly established standards.

Mind-readers are insecure and immature but must be challenged by supernatural interventions to see themselves as they truly are. They must allow the Holy Spirit to bring out the pure spiritual gifts that are embedded in their souls.

Isaiah 33:22 (KVJ) states, "For the Lord is our judge, the Lord is our lawgiver, the Lord is our King, He will save us."

(See also, Romans 14:13, Matthew 7:1–4; Matthew 15:1–20; Job 33:14–18.)

Prayer

Father, there is none like You. You are faithful in holiness and purity, I ask You to instill in us the attitude of humility in order to grow into the image of Your dear Son, Jesus Christ. Amen!

WEEK 44

SUBSTANCE

Seeds that we sow in the soil of the inner man established only by our Creator bring

Understanding that the gifts given to us by God must be developed and protected. With His favor He

Brings us to the windows and doors of opportunities for us to shine for Him. When we follow His lead, He

Secures and stabilizes our position in Him with the anointing that He placed on our lives.

Transcending beyond all human barriers and prejudices we find ourselves strategically placed by God as He

Allows us to impart wisdom and knowledge that He so gracefully breathes into our spirit to meet the

Needs of His precious children.

Constantly our provider refurbishes us with the wellspring of life that never runs dry.

Effectively and efficiently, the Holy Spirit draws people to Himself as we allow Him to empower us for the ministry He called us to, for His honor and glory.

Romans 14:12 (KVJ) states, "So then, everyone, of us shall give account of himself to God."

(See also, 1 Peter 4:10–11;1 Timothy 6:17–21.)

Prayer

You are my Lord. My hope and strength come from You. Thank you for grace and favor that come only from You. Teach me Your ways and give me the discipline to follow You. In Jesus' name. Amen.

<u>Secure Your Joy</u>

Have you been lied to, cheated on and betrayed?

Does the road you now travel on feel like it is paved with thorns?

Have you spent sleepless nights with streams of tears making your vision foggy?

Don't listen to the voice of the enemy nor believe his degrading words and lies.

Tell yourself that you will not believe the report of your friends who have become tools for the enemy of souls.

Stand firm on the word of God because the joy of the Lord is your strength.

Rise up and secure your joy!

Nehemiah 8:10 (KJV) states, "Then he said unto them, Go your way, eat the fat, and drink the sweet, and send portions unto them for whom nothing is prepared, for this day is holy unto our Lord, neither be sorry, for the joy of the Lord is your strength."

(See also, Psalm16:11; Psalm 30:5; Isaiah 61:3; John 15:11; 1 John 1:4.)

<u>Prayer</u>
Lord, You are the strength of my life and my source of joy. Everything that is good comes from You, and that is the reason my hope is in You only. Amen!

WEEK 45

TIME

Time waits for no one because it emanates from the supernatural.

It is a privilege and an opportunity given to us by God.

Moment by moment, as the secrets of the future unfold themselves, we have to seize every second and every minute to do the will of the Creator, since He is the

Essence of time.

Esther 4:14 (NIV) "For if you remain silent at this time, relief and deliverance for the Jews will arise from another place, but you and your father's family will perish. And who knows but that you have come to royal position for such a time as this?"

(See also, Hosea 10:12).

Prayer
My Lord and Savior, please help me recognize windows and doors of opportunities when You open them, so that I will not procrastinate or waiver from my responsibilities and miss Your favor and blessings. Give me the wisdom to choose the correct approach and method. In Jesus' name. Amen!

My Times Are in Your Hands

With every breath that I breathe,

In every step that I take,

For every next heartbeat,

For every waking hour,

Through every mountain and every valley experience,

During every slip and slide,

From project to project,

In its beginning and its end, phase by phase,

From victory to victory, failure to success,

From minor to major, and glory to glory,

Surely, my times are in Your hands.

Lord, You, are in control.

Psalm 31:15 (NIV) states, "My times are in your hands; deliver me from my enemies and from those who pursue me."

(See also, Psalm 89:47; 1 Corinthians 7:29.)

Prayer
Loving Father, although we sometimes give the impression that we really know what we are doing because we think positively. Truly, only You know our future. Teach us to never forget that You are the future, and to seek You in all our endeavors. In the Strong name of Jesus. Amen!

WEEK 46

Don't Sweat the Small Stuff

Why should you be consumed with issues that you cannot control?

Why waste precious moments by being preoccupied with circumstances that you cannot change?

Why spend sleepless nights trying to play mental gymnastics when God has already prepared the way for you?

Why jeopardize your physical and mental status by reciting over and over the wrongs done against you, while the wrong-doers are enjoying their moments by working on making themselves healthy?

Why not focus on important values that will build your relationship with the Lord of your life, your Creator, your family and friends?

Secure every moment by daily, enjoying the gifts that God has given you.

Then you will find that, sweating the small stuff will rob you of precious jewels of time and the value of each day.

Philippians 4:4–7 (NIV) states, "Rejoice in the Lord always. I will say it again: Rejoice! Let your gentleness be evident to all. The Lord is near. Do not be anxious about anything, but in everything, by prayer and petition, with thanksgiving, present your requests to God. And the peace of God, which transcends all understanding, will guard your hearts and minds in Christ Jesus."

(See also Matthew 11:28-30; Hebrews 4:10-13.)

Prayer

Dear Lord, please let me turn my eyes and look steadfastly at You, so that trivialities will grow dim in the light of Your glory and grace. Amen.

SANCTIFICATION IS

Dying to selfish desires and being set apart
    by the Holy Spirit for the use and glory of God.

Having Jesus as the center of our attention
    and source of our joy, even when we feel
    as if we are trampled to the ground.

Seeking to express God's love to the down-and-out,
    the forsaken and the forgotten.

Living a life of integrity without wavering, even
    when it's convenient to fulfill one's greed for
    material possessions and fleeting pleasures.

Being quick to share the good news of Jesus,
    the Savior of the world, who has elected
    us because He loves us.

Choosing to have a great day and counting our blessings
    one by one, despite the bad news that we hear.

Preferring others above ourselves for the cause of the
    Gospel, in order to win souls for the kingdom of God.

Laying aside the weight, cares, and burdens,
    and run this race of life with our minds set on heaven,
    where we'll experience complete sanctification.

1 Thessalonians 5:23 (NIV®) states, "May God himself, the God of peace, sanctify you through and through. May your whole spirit, soul and body be kept blameless at the coming of our Lord Jesus Christ."

Hebrews 13:5-14 (NIV) states, "Keep your lives free from the love of money and be content with what you have, because God has said, 'Never will I leave you; never will I forsake you.' So, we say with confidence, 'The Lord is my helper; I will not be afraid. What can man do to me?' Remember your leaders, who spoke the word of God to you. Consider the outcome of their way of life and imitate their faith. Jesus Christ is the same yesterday and today and forever. Do not be carried away by all kinds of strange teachings. It is good for our hearts to be strengthened by grace, not by ceremonial foods, which are of no value to those who eat them. We have an altar from which those who minister at the tabernacle have no right to eat. The high priest carries the blood of animals into the Most Holy Place as a sin offering, but the bodies are burned outside the camp. And so Jesus also suffered outside the city gate to make the people holy through his own blood. Let us, then, go to him outside the camp, bearing the disgrace he bore. For here we do not have an enduring city, but we are looking for the city that is to come."

(See also, 2Thessalonians 2:13–17.)

Prayer

Father God, You, are all I need. Cause me to crucify my fleshly, selfish desires daily and seek to do Your will always. You satisfy my longing like nothing else can do. I praise You with my whole being. Bless your name. Amen!

WEEK 47

FOCUS ON THE FUTURE

Follow without hesitation and stay focused on the

Undefiled word of God because it is the eternal

Truth manifested in Jesus, the

Undeniable, ever-living Son of God.

Reach out beyond your carnal nature for the living hope that does not fade.

Eternity is promised to those who never give up in the trial of their faith. So, rejoice because the future is bright with the Son that never sets.

1 Peter 1:3–4, 7 (NIV) states, "Praise be to the God and Father of our Lord Jesus Christ! In his great mercy he has given us new birth into a living hope through the resurrection of Jesus Christ from the dead, and into an inheritance that can never perish, spoil or fade—kept in heaven for you, These have come so that your faith—of greater worth than gold, which perishes even though refined by fire—may be proved genuine and may result in praise, glory and honor when Jesus Christ is revealed."

2 Corinthians 4:17–18 (NIV®) states, "For our light and momentary troubles are achieving for us an eternal glory that far outweighs them all. So, we fix our eyes not on what is seen, but on what is unseen. For what is seen is temporary, but what is unseen is eternal."

Prayer

You are Lord God, and there is none like You. I love You, Lord, and I lift my voice to You this day. Thank you for the undeniable hope that comes from You as an inheritance for us who are set apart for You. Teach us how to seize opportunities to win souls for the kingdom of God so they will experience this lively hope. I bless Your name forever. Amen!

NEVER GIVE UP, YOU ARE PRECIOUS

God sees you through the transforming
Power of His Son, Jesus.
Therefore, you are:

The **A**pple of His eye.
His **B**eloved and blessed bride of Christ.
    Chosen and creative steward, who never says, "I can't," to her Lord.
    Daughter of destiny who discerns good and evil.
    Elect lady who assumes her responsibility with confidence.
    Faithful child who seeks to please her Maker.
    Gracious representative of her Savior.
    Honest and humble daughter who leads a life of godly integrity.
    Intelligent creation who knows how to choose her battles.
    Justified by faith and joint heir with Jesus.
    Keen observer who sees others through God's eyes.
    Light in this dark world that extends forgiveness and mercy.
    Messenger of good news.
    New creation through the shed blood of Jesus.
    Overcomer in all circumstances.
    Prized possession as a valuable trophy and precious gem.
    Quality synonymous with the excellency of Christ.
    Royal princess adorned to represent her Prince of Peace.
    Sanctified disciple set apart as an instrument for His use.
    Trusted soldier armored for warfare.
    United with the saints of God.
    Victorious over fleshy destructive desires.
    Wise woman who acts appropriately at the right time and place.
    X-ray of the contents in her heart to ensure there is no wickedness.
    Yoked to the Trinity.
    Zealous in proclaiming the goodness of the Lord in the land of the living.

Proverbs 31:25–26 (NIV) states, "She is clothed with strength and dignity; she can laugh at the days to come. She speaks with wisdom, and faithful instruction is on her tongue." (See also, Proverbs 12:17; Matthew 5:14–16; Romans 8:37; John 15:13–16; 1 Corinthians 6:11.)

<u>Prayer</u>
Loving Lord and Master of my life, I am in awe of Your majesty and perfection. I truly thank you for being everything to me. You gave me purpose and destiny to live for, which became much clearer to me when You removed the scales from my eyes. Thank you, Lord, for the value You placed in me. Cause me to impart words of wisdom to others from the intimacy You share with me. Amen!

WEEK 48

BE STILL AND KNOW THAT HE IS GOD

When life's challenges become unbearable, and you feel like giving up and not caring about the ripple effects of quitting,

Be still and know that He is God, "your Burden-Bearer" so, never give up.

When you have traveled long on life's winding pathways and your good intentions and words of encouragement are manipulated and twisted by others to become punitive,

Be still and know that He is God, "your Sanctifier" so, never give up.

When you become emotionally exhausted and bruised as a result of constant badgering that comes from fault-finding, cynicism and presumptions,

Be still and know that He is God, "your Vindicator and Rewarder" so, never give up.

When all your efforts are utilized as God's instruments to help others, are taken for granted and evil spoken of, or ignored by the recipients you are assigned to help,

Be still and know that he is God, "your Rewarder" and never give up.

Psalm 68:19 states, "Praise be to the Lord, to God our Savior, who daily bears our burdens."

(See also, Job 13:16–18; 1 Corinthians 6:11.)

Prayer

Thank you, Lord God, my heavenly Father because Your promises never fail. Your guaranteed promises assure me that, you are my Burden-bearer, my Sanctifier, my Vindicator and my Rewarder. There is certainly life and spirit in Your words. Therefore, I deeply appreciate Your constant reassurance of Your love from day-to-day that strengthens me in all variations of life's experiences. I shall praise You while I live. Amen!

FAITH

Faith is,
Falling in love with Jesus and spending quality time with Him
in good times and bad times, when it seems like
there are no positive answers to questions.

Faith is,
Allowing Him to lead the way with perfect precision through
life's circumstances as He lovingly pulls us through
our seasons of struggles to bring us to the expected end.

Faith is,
Initiating a God-given confidence with knowledge of His will
to approach the future knowing that our steps are ordered by God.
So, hope and assurance become our songs and the theme of our
conversations.

Faith is,
Trusting and obeying God's precepts and principles
to develop our character as we conform to His image
because the battle we fight daily is a spiritual one.

Faith is,
Having peace in our soul and a song of joy during
the working and waiting periods when it appears like we
will never
see God's blessings and benefits become real in our life.

Faith is,
Believing that
God does not and cannot lie.

Matthew 17:20 (NIV) States, "He replied, 'Because you have so little faith, I tell you the truth, if you have faith as small as a mustard seed, you can say to this mountain,' "Move from here to there," 'and it will move. Nothing will be impossible for you.' "

(See also, Romans 1:17; Romans 5:1–2; Philippians 3:7–10; Hebrews 10:19–23.)

<u>Prayer</u>

How great You are, my trusting Father. I love and appreciate You for being my confidant and never-failing Lord. Today, and always, I trust You with my life and for the pathway through which You lead me. Please give me the sensitivity to recognize You in all circumstances, because I desire to do Your will. Amen!

WEEK 49

GOD IS ABLE

When it seems like there is darkness all around
And the hope of light penetrating seems far-fetched,
God can turn the darkness into perfect sunshine.

Struggles and uncertainties about the future
haunt you day and night, with no relief
in sight, but God can unravel
the knots and free the soul.

When the leviathan spirit raises its head
and manipulates the servants of God to
belittle and suppress the gifts God provided for the building
of His Kingdom, God can preserve and protect His elect.

Disappointment and betrayal become a plague,
day in and day out, causing the emotions to
ride a roller coaster in the mental faculties
with no stopping in sight, but God is able
to eliminate that instability.

God can turn sorrows and tears
into opportunities that lead to joy and laughter,
peace and contentment.
Because God cannot lie, He guarantees
that the humble will receive great grace
and shall persevere through trials.

God will fortify the peacemakers
with His bountiful blessings, internally
and externally because the Prince
of Peace is their everlasting portion and

the song of deliverance and hope is their theme.

Morning shall come with the beautiful sunrise
after the pitch darkness of midnight of the soul
comes to an end. Then a new chapter
in the book of this earthly realm will
begin, never to walk along those corridors
again, because my God will carry
me on eagle's wings while I sing,
"Hallelujah to Jesus my King."

Psalm 27:13–14 (NIV) states, "I am confident of this: I will see the goodness of the Lord in the land of the living. Wait for the Lord; be strong and take heart and wait for the Lord."

(See also, Romans 15:13, Philippians 3:20–21.)

Prayer

You are worthy, O my Father, to receive honor, glory, dominion and power. Yes, You, are glorious and above all things because You are our Creator. Nothing is impossible for You. Give us Your power to persist and stay focused on the goal that is established in You. Yours is the Kingdom, so let it be done here on Earth as it is in Heaven. In Jesus' name. Amen!

Worship, Evangelism, Discipleship

Worship the Lord in the beauty of holiness,
    with your whole being as we come
    into His presence with clean hands
    and pure hearts.
    Bow on your knees before Him with adoration.
    Reverence His majesty because
    our everlasting God and King created
    us to worship Him.

Evangelism is the key that opens the door
    to salvation of lost souls.
    Go into the world and share the good
    news that Jesus gives eternal life and
    lead them to the saving knowledge of
    Jesus Christ, the Savior of humanity.

Discipleship is the pathway that outlines the
    lifestyle Jesus taught us to live by.
    As followers of Christ, we are called
    to be committed to humble services,
    doing the will of God, loving one
    another and making disciples of
    all nations.

John 4:24 (NIV) states, "God is a spirit and His worshipers must worship Him in spirit and in truth."

Matthew 28:19–20 (NIV) states, "Therefore, go and make disciples of all nations baptizing them in the name of the Father and the Son and of the Holy Spirit, and teaching them to obey everything I commanded you. And surely, I am with you always, to the very end of the age."

John 3:34-35 states, "A new command I give to you. Love as I have loved you, so you must love one another. By this all men will know that you are my disciples if you love one another."

<u>Prayer</u>

Thank you, Lord, for the opportunities to be Your extended hands by showing Your unconditional love in what we say and do for people who are neglected, abandoned and rejected. Give us the wisdom and the boldness to speak words of life and healing. Thank you for the resources to provide food and clothing for the needy. Thank you for the courage to lead lost souls to You. You are the way, the truth and the life. In Jesus' name. Amen!

WEEK 50

What Is Freedom?

Freedom is,
Knowing that God is the author
and finisher of your faith and conscientiously,
wearing the garment of praise for the spirit of heaviness.

Freedom is,
Putting faith to work daily, in your lifestyle
while you trust God to unfold in a timely manner, the
specific plans he has for you.

Freedom is,
Having the undisputed assurance that being
a peacemaker who sows peace, raises
a harvest of righteousness.

Freedom is,
Staying in the presence of God to be refreshed and
experience the rest and courage that comes
with pressing into the image of Jesus while investing
quality time with Him.

Freedom is,
Overcoming sinful attacks of the
enemy who comes to kill, steal and destroy,
by declaring the blood of the Lamb,
the word of your testimony and
the sword of the spirit over your life.

Freedom is,
Persevering when it seems like
circumstances cloud your vision and

deafen your spiritual ears, but still
being faithful to your calling, in the face
of destructive criticisms, ridicule and abuse.

Freedom is,
Abiding in the fruit of the spirit, love, which
is a refuge where the enemy cannot
thrive because what we feed will grow
and what we starve will die.

Freedom is,
Knowing that God made us overcomers
and more than conquerors in His Son,
Jesus so that we will not give up on
the faith-walk when the battles of
life's challenges become fierce.

Freedom is,
Getting out of bed every day and walking
in patience and discipline, even though
you do not know how or when God
will put an end to the ungodly issues
that attempt to derail His elect from
their God-ordained destiny.

Freedom is,
Letting go of dreams that have gone unfulfilled
and no longer weeping about the empty places
in life that remain barren. Such decisions
come with a release of peace that brings
about an unexplainable satisfaction, because
letting go was timely, engineered by God through
the power of His word.

2 Corinthians 3:16–18 (NIV) states, "But whenever anyone turns to the Lord, the veil is taken away. Now the Lord is the Spirit, and

where the Spirit of the Lord is, there is freedom. And we who with unveiled faces all reflect the Lord's glory, are being transformed into His likeness with ever-increasing glory, which comes from the Lord, who is the Spirit."

(See also, John 8:31-36; Romans 8:18-21)

<u>Prayer</u>
Glorious Father, Mighty God and King of kings, thank you for the freedom we have in Jesus. He became a prisoner for us to be free. He paid the debt He did not owe, and we could not pay. Thank you for removing the veil from our eyes so we can experience His glory because there is where we find freedom. In Jesus' name. Amen!

Be Still My Soul

When there is pitch darkness in the
midnight of the soul because Jesus
gives a song that bubbles up from
the heart through the lips of the
believer, "The Lord is my light and
my salvation, I shall not be afraid."

Be Still My Soul
When the unceasing struggles of life's
issues disrupt the smooth flow of a
peaceful environment and the waves
of temptations shudder the helm of your spirit,
Jesus is the one who stills the storm.

Be Still My Soul
When the enemy sets roadblocks on the
journey to the celestial city and attempts
to sidetrack you from your heavenly calling.
Remember that God is sovereign and
He does all things well for your good
and for His glory.

Be Still My Soul
And be patient while God is working on your
Behalf, minute by minute, hour by hour, day by day.
He is God, He never fails and cannot lie.
O my soul, rest in the Lord and be
refreshed with the ever-flowing water
that never runs dry, because in due
season you shall reap the harvest of
God's will for your life.

Psalm 46:10 (NIV) states, "Be still and know that I am God; I will be exalted among the nations, I will be exalted in the earth."

(See also, Psalm 37:7–8; Psalm 89:9).

<u>Prayer</u>
Lord, You, are the love of my life because I can depend on You always. Thanks for your grace that undergirds me in all circumstances of life. You are the absolute promise-keeper. I bless Your name at all times. Amen!

Week 51

God Can Heal the Broken-Hearted

If you develop an intimate relationship
With Jesus, He will create the
Supernatural ability in your spirit
To forgive those who repeatedly,
Emotionally and physically, abuse you
Because the events of time did not
Flow according to their expectations.

If you focus on God's grace and mercy
Towards you daily, you will
Understand and have the assurance that
He is holding you in the palm of His
Hands and protecting you from mental derangement.

If you allow your heart to sing
Praises to your heavenly Father and
Seek His face, the light of His
Countenance will reflect in your
Spirit and the spiritual surgery
Of the Great Physician will heal
The shattered and broken pieces that
Seemingly, can never be mended.

If you remain sensitive and
Obedient to His will, He shall
Open the doors that lead to
The path of escape into
His green pastures where
There is sweet peace, joy
And freedom as you bask
In the glory of His presence.

Psalm 147:3 (NIV) states, "He heals the broken-hearted and binds up their wounds."

Psalm 23:2–3 (NIV) states, "He makes me lie down in green pastures, He leads me beside quiet waters, He restores my soul. He guides me in the path of righteousness for His name's sake."

(See also, Exodus 15:26.)

<u>Prayer</u>

Father, it is in Your precious Son's holy name that I come to You, expressing my gratitude to You for allowing Him to take the beatings that inflicted wounds in his body so that I could be healed. By His stripes I am healed. I confess that I am healed because the Lord bound up my emotional wounds and gave me a healthy heart, as if it were never broken. Glory to God! Amen!

Trust God, Always

Troublesome times have a tendency
to pull at our heartstrings and
cause us to take on a depressive spirit,
but during those times God will

Reach out to us and extend His loving
arms around us, lay our head on
His breast, so we can hear his heartbeat
saying, "I love you."

Understand and believe God's promise,
that He would never leave you nor forsake you,
is like invaluable precious diamonds
that will never change.
Stand firm and not waiver from God's
precepts because they are refreshing
to the spirit and healing to the
bruised and broken.

Take all the issues of this fleeting life
and cast them on the Lord, not withholding
anything because He cares for you.
He is the bearer of your burdens
So, let go and let Him take control.

Proverbs 3:5–6 (NIV) states, "Trust in the Lord with all your heart and lean not on your own understanding and he will make your path straight."

Hebrews 2:12–13a (NIV) states, "He says, 'I will declare your name to my brothers; in the presence of the congregation I will sing your praises.' And again, I will put my trust in Him."

Prayer

Dear Lord, today I give You my all, withholding nothing, because You created me. You know me more than anyone else, so nothing can be hidden from You. Let Your will be done, and Your kingdom come in my life. In Jesus' name. Amen!

WEEK 52

YOU CAN DEPEND ON GOD

When it seems like there is no end to
the winding road with its rocky
slopes, you can depend on God to help
you through those rough paths.

When doubts and uncertainties plague
you day after day and you wonder
how far away the day of breakthrough is,
You can depend on God to bring
peace to those mental gymnastics.

When in the stillness of the night, the
tempter comes to you at your most
vulnerable moment, you can depend
on God to speak gently to your spirit,
"Listen to me. Wait for me. I am with you."

When your spirit is crushed and no one
sees the bleeding heart, you can
depend on God to give you the
attitude of forgiveness as you experience
His love, tenderness and healing.

Psalm 62:7–8 (NIV) states, "My salvation and my honor depend on God; He is my mighty rock, my refuge. Trust in him at all times, O people pour out your heart to him, for God is our refuge."

(See also, Joshua 1:5; John 14:18.)

Prayer

Dear Lord, You, are my confidence and my strong tower. Thank you for the assurance that You will never leave me or forsake me. Teach me to wait for Your perfect timing that will bring me rest and satisfaction. In Jesus' name. Amen!

You Are Lord God Almighty

You are sovereign and totally in charge
of the whole universe and everything
that exists in it because You spoke
them into being; therefore You
must be awed, reverenced
and worshipped.

You protect Your beloved and elect
in the face of adversity.
You bring justice to the hypocrite
who has a form of godliness
because You will not be mocked.

You are the Almighty and You will bring
to nothing the carnal minded
that manipulates Your precious
life-giving word to satisfy
self-aggrandizement.

You are the Supreme Father who cradles
the broken-hearted in Your loving arms
and prevents the enemy of their souls from
inflicting anymore harm.

Genesis 1:27 (NIV) states, "So God created man in his own image, in the image of God he created him; male and female, he created them."

Leviticus 20:7 (NIV) states, "Consecrate yourselves and be holy because I am the Lord your God."

Prayer

Great God of Heaven and Earth, I praise and adore You for who You are. You are the all-powerful one. You are all-knowing and present in all places all times. Nothing is a surprise to You. You are the one who makes us holy, so I give all my uncertainties to You and trust You for my future in Jesus' name. Amen!

Stay on Track

Be steadfast and stay focused
on your goal, which is in Christ Jesus,
who called and anointed you to
spread the good news of His
love for mankind.

Do not be distracted by the
manipulative tactics of the enemy
who works overtime, to distract
you from your God-ordained destiny.
Listen to the voice of the spirit and follow
His divine lead.

Be discerning and watchful for
the tide of the times that could
scoop you up into oblivion, a place
where your identity and self-esteem
will be swept away into the depth
of depression and despair.

Do not accept less than God's
best for you, neither the lies of the enemy
that echo in your mind intermittently,
in the stillness of the moment.
God has made you more than a conqueror,
with no exception, so soar like an eagle
and free yourself from the chains around your neck.

Isaiah 26:3–4 (NIV) states, "You will keep in perfect peace, those whose minds are steadfast, because they trust in you. Trust in the Lord forever, for the Lord himself, is the Rock eternal.")

Peter 5:10 (NIV) states, "And the God of all grace, who called you to his eternal glory in Christ, after you have suffered a little while will himself restore you and make you strong, firm and steadfast."

Prayer

Glory to our Mighty God who reigns forever! Father, You, are concerned about every aspect of our lives. There is nothing strange or new for You. You knew from the beginning, every step that we would take in this journey of life and You watched over us and guarded us with Your grace in the time of need. Thank you for Your protection, provision and providence. In the holy name of Jesus. Amen!

DELIVERANCE

Dare to make the decision to obey God's word,

Even when it may cause separation from others.

Loving God and obeying His will always leads to the correct path.

Inspirations from the Holy Spirit will clarify that which seems dim.

Victory is sweet when we follow God's prescriptions.

Every day is a new gift from our Creator, God our Provider.

Revival is embedded in deliverance because of the refreshing that comes from the Living Water.

Activate and stir-up the gifts buried in you for so long.

No experience during the midnight of the soul, should be taken for granted because God will turn it around for your good and His glory.

Courage comes from your God-given strength because you spend time with your Savior.

Encourage yourself with songs of deliverance and experience overflowing joy during your journey to your destiny.

Psalm 34:4-7 (NIV®Text) "I sought the Lord and he answered me; he delivered me from all my fears. Those who look to him are radiant; their faces are never covered with shame. This poor man called, and the Lord heard him; he saved him out of all his troubles. The angel of the Lord encamps around those who fear him, and he delivers them".
(See also Matthew 6:5-15; 2 Corinthians 1:1-11.)

Prayer

Thank you, Father for the air that I breathe. I appreciate you for sending Jesus, your only son who took my place, to be crucified as a criminal for all the wrongs that I have done and what I will do, that I am oblivious to. Thank you for being such a God of love and mercy. You delivered me because I sought you in the name that is above every other name, JESUS! He rose from the dead so that I am, able to receive everlasting life with the ultimate and complete deliverance from this dark world, while reigning with Him! AMEN!

PATIENCE

Patience, a dynamic virtue and fruit of the Holy Spirit, grows when it is tested and overcomes.

Actions and attitudes of the tested, reveal rest in God and peace that surpasses human understanding.

Trials appear but self-control becomes unmoved and brings the tried to their knees, to wait for the day of vindication and victory to arrive.

Inspirations from the Word of God give strength to endure with a song in the heart and praise to Jehovah from the lips.

Evening comes and the sun sets, so the flash-back of trials appear, but shouts of joy from His presence resound from the inner-person into the atmosphere.

Notification to the enemy of our souls who comes to kill, steal and destroy, that we overcome by the blood of the Lamb and the word of our testimony.

Casting all cares into the hands of our Savior because He cares for every aspect of our lives, we'll find freedom from the chains that entangle us.

Enthusiasm mixed with humility becomes the new order of the day, because the willingness to treat others with patience is an attitude ordained by God, since what we, "Sow, that shall we also reap? Patience sowed results in a harvest of patience.

Proverbs 19:11 (NIV®Text) states, "A man's wisdom gives him patience, it is to his glory to overlook an offense."

Galatians 5:22-23 (NIV®Text) states, "But the fruit of the Spirit is love, joy, peace, patience, kindness, goodness, faithfulness, gentleness and self-control. Against such there is no law."

(See also Ecclesiastes 7:8; Colossians 1:11; 2 Timothy 4:2.)

<u>Prayer</u>

My Abba, it is in the strong name of Jesus that I come in your presence. I know you care about every aspect of my life. Cause me to represent my Messiah throughout my life's journey, as I follow His lead and grow more in His love and exercise patience on a daily basis. Amen! Amen!

THE IN-BETWEEN TIMES

Have you ever felt like you've been positioned smack in the middle of the in-between times? Those times when you wonder whether you are "going" or "coming" as you try to keep up with your daily schedules in the midst of an internal war.

The in-between times are those periods when you felt like that season would pass and it would only be a memory or dream that produces laughter or teardrops of joy. Then suddenly, the battle of challenges becomes fierce.

Have you ever felt that victory is just around the bend? But, Oh! Here comes a surprise…you faced a disappointing discovery which propelled you to your knees and forced you to spend time in the presence of the Lover of your soul, Jesus.

You are then left with no alternative but to listen to Him during these in-between times, as He whispers with words of reassurance,
"Be still and know that I am God."

Could these in-between times be named, the period of "character building"?
This waiting process enveloped in time, can result in developing the fruit of the spirit: patience, forbearance, and temperance.
Yes, waiting with an expectancy for answers to days,
weeks, months,
and years of prayers and supplication.

The in-between times are those gaps of time between the day, a seed was planted and the day of harvesting its crop. It is during these gaps of time, we must weed and feed it regularly, and check the growth process to ensure that the conditions for healthy growth are being maintained until the day of harvest.

It is during those in-between times you dare not make the mistake of uprooting the new growths, thinking they are weeds.

Therefore, be gentle, cautious, and wise in choosing your words. Listen well and do not assume, nor be judgmental, critical or cynical. If not, you may tragically uproot
new healthy growth or good seeds you planted.
Trust God to carry you through the in-between times and you will experience rest and peace in Him.

Psalm 27:13-14 (NIV®Text) states, "I am still confident of this; I will see the goodness of the Lord in the land of the living. Wait for the Lord; be strong and take heart and wait for the Lord."

Psalm 130:5-6 (NIV®Text) states, "I wait for the Lord, my soul waits and in his word I put my hope. My soul waits, and in his word I put my hope. My soul waits for the Lord more than watchmen wait for the morning."

Hosea 10:12 (NIV®Text) states, "Sow for yourselves righteousness, reap the fruit of unfailing love and break up your unplowed ground; for it is time to seek the Lord, until he comes and showers righteousness on you."

(See also, Isaiah 30:18-22; Hebrews 9:24-28; James 3:17-18.)

Prayer
Dear Lord, I honor and adore you! I praise you with my whole being! My soul mind and spirit seek after you because I live and breathe in your presence. My hope is in you. You promised if I hope in you, I would be like Mount Zion. I truly receive that promise. Lord I lift your name on high. In Jesus' mighty and glorious name. Amen!

Topical Index

A
Accountability 144
Alone with God 99
Anger 42
Anointing 125
Are You a Giver or a Taker? 146
Are you Ready? 10

B
Be still and know He is God 184
Be Still My Soul 195
Being Secure in Christ Guarantees Success 119
Beloved 73
Breakthrough 101
Bring Us down Lord 102

C
Change 37
Clean Hands 165
Consecrate Your Members 38

D
Declaration of Who I am 133
Declaration of a Woman of Integrity 97
Declaration of God's Elect Lady 32
Declaration of God's Glory in your life 110
Deliverance 207
Destiny 4
Discipline 135
Divert Me, O God 156
Don't Sweat the Small Stuff 177

E
Easter is for our Redemption 116
Emotional Abuse is not of God 46
Enter His Presence 152

F
Faith 186
Fault-Finding 154
Fishers of Men 95
Focus on the Future 180
F-O-R-G-I-V-E-N-E-S-S 34
Forgiveness Is 34
Fragrance 92

G
Give God a Chance in Your Life 90
God Can Heal the Broken-Hearted 197
God is a God of New Beginnings 89
God is Able 188
God is my Vindicator 177
Grace 36
Guide Me 87

H
Hallelujah Anyhow 30
Happiness Is 85
H-E-L-P-E-R 162
His Majesty 148
Holy Spirit you are Welcome in my Life 130
Honor 84
Hope 81
How to Invoke Respect 143
Humility is the Key 82

I
I am God's Child 40
I Shall Prevail 78
Integrity 96

J
Jesus is The Gate 77
Jesus, I'm in Need 79
Jesus, You are the Greatest Husband 11

L
Light 29
Living a Lifestyle with the Alphabet of Praise 26
Love Is... 70
Love Never Fails 72
Lover 74

M
M.A.N 64
Man- The Human Race 68
Man Born of Woman is Full of Trouble 67
M-E-E-K-N-E-S-S 20
Meekness Is... 22
Mind Readers 170
My Times Are in Your Hands 176

O
Obedience 62
Offence 141

P
P-A-S-S-I-O-N 93
Patience 209
Peace 61
Pray 24
Preserve Me 17
Prosperity 18
Purify me, O God 15

R
Redemption 158
Revival 160

S
Sanctification Is...178
Satisfaction 59
Secure Your Joy 174
Serve God 142
Show Me An Angry Person 43
Stand 111
Stay on Track 205
Stewardship 57
Submit 14

Substance 172
Successful Transition Takes Time 12
Surrender 113

T
Tears 137
Thanks 112
The Blood of Jesus 114
The Glory of Them All 55
The In-Between Times 211
The Intangible 106
The Journey Is Rough But....163
The Leviathan Spirit 167
The Lord is my Protection 53
The P.O.S of God (The Eagle) 10
The Sanctuary of God 150
The Truth About Fatherhood 66
Thoughts 139
T-I-M-E 175
Tongue 12
Trust God Always 199

V
Victory 8

W
Wait 51
Wake Up 127
Walking in God's Will 6
Walking in Your Destiny 3
What is Freedom? 192
What Is Meekness? 20
What is Strength? 1
What will you do with this man, Jesus? 48

Woman 132
Words 121
Worship, Evangelism, Discipleship 190

Y
You are Lord God Almighty 203
You are my Refuge and Strength 16
You are the Glory & the Lifter of My Head 108
You Can Depend on God 201
Your Love Constrains and Restrains Me 75

CPSIA information can be obtained
at www.ICGtesting.com
Printed in the USA
LVHW010342190721
693040LV00010B/49